2nd Shared Task on Discourse Relation Parsing and Treebanking (DISRPT 2021)

Punta Cana, Dominican Republic
11 November 2021

Editors:

Amir Zeldes
Yang Janet Liu
Mike Iruskieta
Philippe Muller
Chloé Braud
Sonia Badene

ISBN: 978-1-7138-9169-7

Printed from e-media with permission by:

Curran Associates, Inc.
57 Morehouse Lane
Red Hook, NY 12571

CURRAN ASSOCIATES INC. proceedings.com

Some format issues inherent in the e-media version may also appear in this print version.

Printed with permission by Curran Associates, Inc. (2024)

For permission requests, please contact the Association for Computational Linguistics at the address below.

Association for Computational Linguistics
209 N. Eighth Street
Stroudsburg, Pennsylvania 18360

Phone: 1-570-476-8006
Fax: 1-570-476-0860

acl@aclweb.org

Additional copies of this publication are available from:

Curran Associates, Inc.
57 Morehouse Lane
Red Hook, NY 12571 USA
Phone: 845-758-0400
Fax: 845-758-2633
Email: curran@proceedings.com
Web: www.proceedings.com

EMNLP 2021

The Shared Task on Discourse Relation Parsing and Treebanking

Proceedings of the 2nd Shared Task on Discourse Relation Parsing and Treebanking (DISRPT 2021)

November 11, 2021
Punta Cana, Dominican Republic

Proceedings of the 2nd Shared Task on Discourse Relation Parsing and Treebanking (DISRPT 2021)

Co-located with CODI 2021

Edited by:

Amir Zeldes, Georgetown University
Yang Janet Liu, Georgetown University
Mikel Iruskieta, University of the Basque Country
Philippe Muller, IRIT Toulouse
Chloé Braud, IRIT-CNRS-ANITI Toulouse
Sonia Badene, Linagora-IRIT

Organizing Committee

Amir Zeldes, Georgetown University
Yang Janet Liu, Georgetown University
Mikel Iruskieta, University of the Basque Country
Philippe Muller, IRIT Toulouse
Chloé Braud, IRIT-CNRS-ANITI Toulouse
Sonia Badene, Linagora-IRIT

Table of Contents

The DISRPT 2021 Shared Task on Elementary Discourse Unit Segmentation, Connective Detection, and Relation Classification
Amir Zeldes, Yang Janet Liu, Mikel Iruskieta, Philippe Muller, Chloé Braud and Sonia Badene . . 1

A Transformer Based Approach towards Identification of Discourse Unit Segments and Connectives
Sahil Bakshi and Dipti Sharma 13

Multi-lingual Discourse Segmentation and Connective Identification: MELODI at Disrpt2021
Morteza Kamaladdini Ezzabady, Philippe Muller and Chloé Braud 22

Delexicalised Multilingual Discourse Segmentation for DISRPT 2021 and Tense, Mood, Voice and Modality Tagging for 11 Languages
Tillmann Dönicke 33

A Unified Approach to Discourse Relation Classification in nine Languages
Hanna Varachkina and Franziska Pannach 46

DisCoDisCo at the DISRPT2021 Shared Task: A System for Discourse Segmentation, Classification, and Connective Detection
Luke Gessler, Shabnam Behzad, Yang Janet Liu, Siyao Peng, Yilun Zhu and Amir Zeldes 51

Conference Program

13:30–13:45 *The DISRPT 2021 Shared Task on Elementary Discourse Unit Segmentation, Connective Detection, and Relation Classification*
Amir Zeldes, Yang Janet Liu, Mikel Iruskieta, Philippe Muller, Chloé Braud and Sonia Badene

13:50–14:20 *A Transformer Based Approach towards Identification of Discourse Unit Segments and Connectives*
Sahil Bakshi and Dipti Sharma

14:20–14:50 *Multi-lingual Discourse Segmentation and Connective Identification: MELODI at Disrpt2021*
Morteza Kamaladdini Ezzabady, Philippe Muller and Chloé Braud

14:50–15:20 *Delexicalised Multilingual Discourse Segmentation for DISRPT 2021 and Tense, Mood, Voice and Modality Tagging for 11 Languages*
Tillmann Dönicke

16:00–16:30 *A Unified Approach to Discourse Relation Classification in nine Languages*
Hanna Varachkina and Franziska Pannach

16:30–17:00 *DisCoDisCo at the DISRPT2021 Shared Task: A System for Discourse Segmentation, Classification, and Connective Detection*
Luke Gessler, Shabnam Behzad, Yang Janet Liu, Siyao Peng, Yilun Zhu and Amir Zeldes

The DISRPT 2021 Shared Task on Elementary Discourse Unit Segmentation, Connective Detection, and Relation Classification *

Amir Zeldes
Georgetown University
az364@georgetown.edu

Yang Janet Liu
Georgetown University
yl879@georgetown.edu

Mikel Iruskieta
University of the Basque Country
mikel.iruskieta@ehu.eus

Philippe Muller
IRIT Toulouse
philippe.muller@irit.fr

Chloé Braud
IRIT-CNRS-ANITI Toulouse
chloe.braud@irit.fr

Sonia Badene
Linagora-IRIT
sbadene@linagora.com

Abstract

In 2021, we organized the second iteration of a shared task dedicated to the underlying units used in discourse parsing across formalisms: the DISRPT Shared Task (**Dis**course **R**elation **P**arsing and **T**reebanking). Adding to the 2019 tasks on Elementary Discourse Unit Segmentation and Connective Detection, this iteration of the Shared Task included for the first time a track on discourse relation classification across three formalisms: RST, SDRT, and PDTB. In this paper we review the data included in the Shared Task, which covers nearly 3 million manually annotated tokens from 16 datasets in 11 languages, survey and compare submitted systems and report on system performance on each task for both annotated and plain-tokenized versions of the data.

1 Introduction

Building on rapid progress in NLP for discourse parsing in the past decade (e.g. Iruskieta et al. 2013, Zhou et al. 2014, Afantenos et al. 2012, Braud et al. 2017, Wang and Lan 2015, Li et al. 2016, Perret et al. 2016), the past two years since the DISRPT 2019 Shared Task (Zeldes et al., 2019) have seen unprecedented performance on benchmark datasets for discourse parsing (e.g. Guz and Carenini 2020; Liu et al. 2020; Kurfali 2020; Zhang et al. 2021b). Following the 2019 Shared Task, our focus in 2021 remained on the most established frameworks for discourse relation treebanking: Rhetorical Structure Theory (Mann and Thompson, 1988), the Penn Discourse Treebank's framework (Prasad et al., 2014), and Segmented Discourse Representation Theory (Asher, 1993).

With the progress achieved on discourse segmentation and connective detection since 2019, this year we decided to extend the competition to a new task: discourse relation classification across frameworks. Although work on relation classification is not new, work has generally been separated into several somewhat independent strands of work: relation classification with explicit connectives (see Kido and Aizawa 2016; Nie et al. 2019), implicit relation classification (Wang and Lan, 2016; Kim et al., 2020), and full discourse constituent (Guz and Carenini, 2020; Zhang et al., 2021b) or dependency parsing (Morey et al., 2018). We believe that these strands of research can come together and benefit from data across frameworks, but only if we are able to formulate a common denominator which poses the problem of discourse relation recognition in similar terms, independently of the underlying theoretical assumptions.

In addition to the new relation classification task, we also updated and expanded the two tasks from 2019 and added a new surprise dataset (and language) which became available in the interim: the Persian RST Corpus (Shahmohammadi et al., 2021).[1] While it remains impossible to place some data openly online due to licensing constraints, all annotations, as well as text for open access datasets, is available from the Shared Task repository,[2] as well as scripts for reconstructing the underlying text for proprietary datasets.

In the next section, we will describe the tasks for this year, starting with the new task of Relation Classification across Frameworks, followed by the existing tasks, followed by Section 3, which provides an overview of the shared task data. Section 4 briefly discusses our effort addressing the ethical and transparency issues related to NLP shared task, inspired by Escartín et al. (2021). Section 5 then describes the Shared Task system submissions and results, followed by a discussion and conclusion.

*Discourse Relation Parsing and Treebanking (DISRPT 2021) was held in conjunction with CODI at EMNLP 2021 in the Dominican Republic and Online (https://sites.google.com/georgetown.edu/disrpt2021).

[1] https://github.com/hadiveisi/PersianRST

[2] https://github.com/disrpt/sharedtask2021

Proceedings of the 2nd Shared Task on Discourse Relation Parsing and Treebanking (DISRPT 2021), pages 1–12
November 11, 2021. ©2021 Association for Computational Linguistics

2 Tasks

2.1 Relation Classification across Frameworks

A major challenge to the goal of enabling relation classification across frameworks is formed by the structural differences between theories: while RST conceptualizes discourse in the form of single rooted, usually projective and hierarchical constituent trees, SDRT assumes an also hierarchical but less constrained graph structure (including multiple relations between units), while PDTB-style corpora assume no overarching macro-structure, with relations applying between independent, possibly overlapping spans of text, which need not cover an entire document. Despite these differences, all frameworks postulate *directed, labeled discourse relations*, and often come to similar and highly correlated insights (cf. Demberg et al. 2019).

In order to represent data across frameworks on an equal footing, we opted to initially convert discourse relation information from RST, PDTB, and SDRT datasets into a set of discourse unit pairs for which a discourse relation (either explicit or implicit) is known to apply. Because only PDTB-style data marks connectives, we chose to integrate these into the argument span within which they were syntactically integrated and restrict the spans involved in the relation to exactly two: `unit1` and `unit2` in text order. However, since PDTB-style data does order argument spans based on relations regardless of text order (to represent cause and effect, etc.), and since SDRT and RST relations are also directed, we retained the direction of the relation in a dedicated field, indicating whether it was a left-to-right relation (`1>2`) or right-to-left (`1<2`).

Additionally, since we wanted to give systems a chance to use as much context as desired, we explicitly included the sentences containing each unit in shared task data, as well as giving stand-off running token IDs for both units and their sentences, which are linked to the numbered tokens from the existing segmentation and connective detection tasks. The resulting format, found in the task's `.rels` files, is shown in Table 1.

The table shows an entry from the English GUM corpus (Zeldes, 2017), part of an interview with a biologist studying ants, in which use of a lot of (ant) colonies is brought as evidence (pointing right-to-left, hence `dir` is `1<2`) that the results of a study are very reliable. The `unit_txt` fields give the space separated tokens in the head unit of each block of discourse units involved in the relation. The first unit 'The results are very reliable' is annotated as discontinuous in the source corpus, as indicated by the reserved token '<*>', which stands in for the missing words 'we got', which can be seen in the full sentence containing this unit, under `unit1_sent`. The second unit is also part of a longer, complex block of units, including a coordinated second piece of evidence (the experiment was blind), and a further nested discourse unit ('wherever possible'), both of which have similar entries for their respective discourse relations elsewhere in the `.rels` data.

As this example shows, context can help to identify relations: in fact, without the containing sentences, we would not know that these are ant colonies, which makes the setting 'experimental study' easier to recognize. Since we did not want to restrict systems to just head units, and conceivably wanted to allow systems to use the entire document if desired, the token offset fields (`unit1_toks`, `s2_toks`, etc.) were given and indicated the position of the relation in the larger text, represented in sequence in the `.tok` and `.conllu` files from the EDU Segmentation and Connective Detection tasks.

For datasets with large numbers of relations and/or very rare relations, we used established collapsing procedures to reduce the number of target relations and ensure that dev and test sets only included relations attested in the training data. In such cases, the original labels are available in the `orig_label` column, and target labels for the shared task are available in the final `label` column.

2.2 EDU Segmentation and Connective Detection

As in the 2019 Shared Task, EDUs and connectives were represented in each corpus in two formats, corresponding to two scenarios: Treebanked data (now named `*.conllu`, previously named `.conll` in 2019), which included an (ideally gold) dependency parse, including gold sentence splits and POS tags, and unannotated, plain tokens (`*.tok`). As in 2019, for datasets that had Universal POS tags and/or UD dependencies, including these was preferred, though we followed the CoNLL-U format's convention of allowing two POS tag fields (UPOS for universal tags, XPOS for language spe-

field	value
doc	GUM_interview_ants
unit1_toks	954-955,958-961
unit2_toks	962-967
unit1_txt	The results <*> are very reliable .
unit2_txt	We had a lot of colonies
s1_toks	954-961
s2_toks	962-982
unit1_sent	The results we got are very reliable .
unit2_sent	We had a lot of colonies containing a lot of ants , and wherever possible we conducted the experiment blind .
dir	1<2
orig_label	evidence
label	evidence

Table 1: An Example of Columns in the Tabular *.rels Data Format for the Relation Classification Task.

```
# sent_id = GUM_interview_stardust-28
# text = Yes [see below].
1    Yes    yes    INTJ   UH     _                                  0  root       _  BeginSeg=Yes
2    [      [      PUNCT  -LSB-  _                                  3  punct      _  BeginSeg=Yes|SpaceAfter=No
3    see    see    VERB   VBP    Mood=Ind|Tense=Pres|VerbForm=Fin   1  parataxis  _  _
4    below  below  ADV    RB     _                                  3  advmod     _  SpaceAfter=No
5    ]      ]      PUNCT  -RSB-  _                                  3  punct      _  SpaceAfter=No
6    .      .      PUNCT  .      _                                  1  punct      _  _

411  Yes    _  _  _  _  _  _  _  BeginSeg=Yes
412  [      _  _  _  _  _  _  _  BeginSeg=Yes
413  see    _  _  _  _  _  _  _  _
414  below  _  _  _  _  _  _  _  _
415  ]      _  _  _  _  _  _  _  _
416  .      _  _  _  _  _  _  _  _
```

Figure 1: Segmentation Format: treebanked (*.conllu, top) and plain (*.tok, bottom)

cific tags), a morphology field with unlimited morphological annotations, and a secondary dependency field for enhanced dependencies where available. The tenth column (MISC in CoNLL-U) was used for gold standard labels and additional annotations (e.g. `SpaceAfter` to indicate whitespace in underlying data), which all followed the CoNLL-U key=value format: `BeginSeg=Yes` for EDU segmentation and BI tags for connectives, `Seg=B-Conn` and `Seg=I-Conn`, versus "_" for unannotated tokens. The second scenario included no annotations except for tokenization and the same document boundary annotations found in the treebanked files. No sentence splits were provided in this scenario. Figure 1 illustrates both formats.

Evaluation scripts were provided for both segmentation and connective detection, with positive class, span-based F-score being the target. As in 2019, for connective detection the evaluation targets only exact matches, meaning that precision and recall are calculated out of the total connective spans (not tokens) available in the gold data, without partial credit or fuzzy matching. As a result, systems identifying the span in (1) below are given one precision error and one recall error, since the prediction misses the gold span and invents one not present in gold data.

(1) Gold: In/B-Conn order/I-Conn to/_
Pred: In/B-Conn order/I-Conn to/I-Conn

3 Shared Task Data

The DISRPT 2021 Shared Task data comprises 16 datasets in 11 languages, 13 of which target elementary discourse unit segmentation, and 3 dedicated to explicit connective annotation, and all 16 being included in the relation classification task. Table 2 gives an overview of the datasets. Of the 16 datasets, training data for 15 were released in their updated 2021 version approximately 3 months before the shared task deadline, while the final one, RST annotations from the Persian RST Corpus, was released as a 'surprise' dataset/language together with all test sets just one month before the announced deadline. For five of the datasets, licensing constraints prevented online publication of the entire underlying texts (e.g. Wall Street Journal material), meaning that the public repository contains only annotations for those corpora, with tokens replaced by underscores. Of these datasets, four contain no text at all (English PDTB and RST-DT, Chinese CDTB, and Turkish TDB), and one (English GUM) contains data for 11/12 genres, but requires download of the text for the 12th genre, Reddit forum discussions.

corpus	language	framework	sentences	tokens	documents	units	segStyle	relations	relTypes	discontinuous
deu.rst.pcc	German	RST	2,193	33,222	176	3,040	EDU	2,164	26	No
eng.rst.gum	English	RST	8,292	152,856	168	19,268	EDU	13,897	23	Yes
eng.rst.rstdt	English	RST	8,318	205,829	385	21,789	EDU	16,002	17	Yes
eng.sdrt.stac	English	SDRT	11,087	52,354	45	12,588	EDU	9,580	16	No
eus.rst.ert	Basque	RST	2,380	45,780	164	4,202	EDU	2,533	29	Yes
fas.rst.prstc	Persian	RST	2,179	66,926	150	5,855	EDU	4,100	17	Yes
fra.sdrt.annodis	French	SDRT	1,507	32,699	86	3,429	EDU	2,185	18	Yes
nld.rst.nldt	Dutch	RST	1,651	24,898	80	2,343	EDU	1,608	32	No
por.rst.cstn	Portuguese	RST	2,221	63,332	140	5,537	EDU	4,148	32	Yes
rus.rst.rrt	Russian	RST	23,044	473,005	332	41,542	EDU	28,868	22	Yes
spa.rst.rststb	Spanish	RST	2,089	58,717	267	3,351	EDU	2,240	28	Yes
spa.rst.sctb	Spanish	RST	516	16,515	50	744	EDU	439	24	Yes
zho.rst.sctb	Mandarin	RST	580	15,496	50	744	EDU	439	26	Yes
corpus	**language**	**framework**	**sentences**	**tokens**	**documents**	**units**	**segStyle**	**relations**	**relTypes**	**discontinuous**
eng.pdtb.pdtb	English	PDTB	48,630	1,156,658	2,162	26,048	Conn	43,920	23	Yes
tur.pdtb.tdb	Turkish	PDTB	31,197	496,358	197	8,748	Conn	2,451	23	Yes
zho.pdtb.cdtb	Mandarin	PDTB	2,891	73,314	164	1,660	Conn	3,657	9	Yes

Table 2: Datasets in the DISRPT 2021 Shared Task.

A script included in the shared task repository was provided in order to reconstruct the data, which requires users to have access to the original LDC releases of the underlying corpora in the case of PDTB, RST-DT, and CDTB or the original Turkish texts available from Middle East Technical University (METU) by request. Missing data for GUM is downloadable directly by running the script and consenting to non-commercial use conditions.

The short names for every dataset begin with an ISO 639-3 three letter code for the language, a framework designation (RST/SDRT/PDTB) and an acronym for the corpus. The names correspond to the following included corpora:

- `deu.rst.pcc` - Potsdam Commentary Corpus (Stede and Neumann, 2014).
- `eng.pdtb.pdtb` - Penn Discourse Treebank (Prasad et al., 2014).
- `eng.rst.gum` - Georgetown University Multilayer corpus (Zeldes, 2017).
- `eng.rst.rstdt` - RST Discourse Treebank (Carlson et al., 2001).
- `eng.sdrt.stac` - Strategic Conversations corpus (Asher et al., 2016).
- `eus.rst.ert` - Basque RST Treebank (Iruskieta et al., 2013).
- `fas.rst.prstc` - Persian RST Corpus (Shahmohammadi et al., 2021).
- `fra.sdrt.annodis` - ANNOtation DIScursive (Afantenos et al., 2012).
- `nld.rst.nldt` - Dutch Discourse Treebank (Redeker et al., 2012).
- `por.rst.cstn` - Cross-document Structure Theory News Corpus (Cardoso et al., 2011).
- `rus.rst.rrt` - Russian RST Treebank (Toldova et al., 2017).
- `spa.rst.rststb` - RST Spanish Treebank (da Cunha et al., 2011).
- `spa.rst.sctb` - RST Spanish-Chinese Treebank (Spanish) (Cao et al., 2018).
- `tur.pdtb.tdb` - Turkish Discourse Bank (Zeyrek and Webber, 2008; Zeyrek and Kurfalı, 2017).
- `zho.pdtb.cdtb` - Chinese Discourse Treebank (Zhou et al., 2014).
- `zho.rst.sctb` - RST Spanish-Chinese Treebank (Chinese) (Cao et al., 2018).

As Table 2 shows, these datasets range from small (under 15,000 tokens for the smallest corpus, zho.rst.sctb), to the larger RST corpora (over 200,000 tokens for RST-DT and the Russian RST Treebank), to the largest PDTB-style datasets (almost half a million tokens for Turkish, and over a million for the English PDTB). The variability in sizes, languages, frameworks, and corpus-specific annotation guidelines were expected to challenge systems, but also promote architectures which can be extended to more languages in the future, and ideally stay robust for low resource settings.

4 Ethical Considerations and Transparency in DISRPT 2021

In the interest of transparency and with inspiration from Escartín et al. (2021), we made efforts to address several ethical and transparency matters in the DISPRT 2021 Shared Task. We created a FAQ page[3] on our main website that laid out information about the Shared Task, participation, equity, and the evaluation criteria etc., which are briefly summarized below.

[3] `https://sites.google.com/georgetown.edu/disrpt2021/faq`

Participation & Organization Generally speaking, we allowed anyone to participate, including the organizers. However, in the interest of transparency and fairness, results from teams which overlap some of the organizers or annotators of any of the included datasets are denoted as such. Though as Escartín et al. (2021) pointed out, there is an understanding that organisers have privileged access to test sets, we pledge that the test data is under strict quarantine until its release and strictly follow this practice. All systems were always rerun and reproduced by evaluators who do not overlap the submission team, and all datasets' original publications had already been made independently of the Shared Task. There are always scenarios where there is overlap between the Shared Task organizers, dataset creators, and participants, and excluding organizer teams may discourage people from organizing future shared tasks, while unfairly penalizing students of organizers who are likely to form the next generation of researchers in the field.

Evaluation & Reproducibility We published the evaluation scripts in the Shared Task GitHub repository[4] at the beginning of the Shared Task for participants to use. We also announced at the beginning of the Shared Task how the overall system rankings in each category will be determined, which is described on the main website. For teams that submitted multiple systems, the best scoring system by macro-averaged F-score on all datasets was selected to represent the team. Moreover, because we believe that code openness and reproducibility are very crucial components in NLP practice, we state up front that all systems must include code to retrain the system from scratch, so that evaluators can test aspects of systems' performance and reproduce reported scores, as well as a detailed README file explaining how to train the system. Systems which cannot be run in the evaluation phase are not be accepted. All submitted systems followed these guidelines, and we were able to retrain and reproduce reported scores falling within the range of multiple random training runs.

Data Access & Resources We are aware that not all teams may have LDC subscriptions. Thus, in the interest of promoting equity regardless of access and funding status, we evaluated submitted systems on the closed LDC datasets for the participants who do not have access to LDC data. We reported scores obtained during the evaluation phase to authors so that they can add them to their papers for the camera-ready version. In addition, resources about each dataset (e.g. papers, annotation manuals etc.) are provided in the README file in each data directory for participants who would like to know more about the corpora used in the shared task.

Negative Results We believe that negative results can bring the field forward, especially when they are accompanied by insightful analysis about why a certain approach does not work. Thus, we encourage such submissions, and their acceptance is subject to the contribution that their analyses can provide to the field. In response to one of the Escartín et al. (2021)'s shared task checklist questions, we allow participants to opt to exclude or anonymize their results in the overall ranking to avoid withdrawal or fear of negative results, though no submission opted for this possibility.

Identification of Annotation Errors We are aware that current machine learning models are capable of catching annotation errors in the original datasets. Thus, we encouraged participants to report such errors to us if they identify any in their error analysis study so that we could pass them along to the original authors of the corpora. In addition, during the data preprocessing stage, we identified and recorded several annotation errors in several corpora. We reported some of these to the original authors earlier this year as they needed to be corrected in order for such annotation instances to be included in the Shared Task. We intend to compile the rest of the annotation errors after the workshop and report them to corpus creators accordingly.

5 Results

For EDU segmentation and connective detection, we report precision, recall, and F1 scores for systems in the two tasks, each consisting of two scenarios: EDU segmentation and connective detection, with treebanked and plain tokenized data; for relation classification the accuracy score is used. The overall system rankings in each category are determined by the macro-average score across treebanks, where each treebank score is decided by the micro-averaged metric.

Five systems were submitted to the shared task, four of which attempted the EDU segmentation

[4] `https://github.com/disrpt/sharedtask2021/tree/main/utils`

corpus	TMVM			DiscoDisco*			disCut*			SegFormers			mean
(treebanked)	P	R	F1	P	R	F1	P	R	F1	P	R	F1	
deu.rst.pcc	94.57	88.78	91.58	97.07	94.15	95.58	98.91	92.52	**95.61**	93.71	96.26	94.97	94.44
eng.rst.gum	94.16	79.86	86.42	93.9	94.43	**94.15**	93.27	93.65	93.46	91.47	95.67	93.52	91.89
eng.rst.rstdt	87.18	65.52	74.81	96.39	96.89	96.64	96.16	95.99	96.08	96.15	98.04	**97.09**	91.16
eng.sdrt.stac	98.73	85.52	91.65	96.25	93.63	94.91	97.41	92.37	94.82	96.73	95.67	**96.20**	94.40
eus.rst.ert	87.23	66.49	75.46	93.42	87.73	**90.46**	90.04	83.11	86.44	87.23	88.65	87.94	85.08
fas.rst.prstc	88.28	74.18	80.62	92.79	93.10	**92.94**	93.54	90.75	92.12	90.53	94.18	92.32	89.50
fra.sdrt.annodis	82.13	49.84	62.03	89.43	90.65	**90.02**	87.26	88.67	87.96	86.76	88.03	87.39	81.85
nld.rst.nldt	95.38	85.50	90.17	97.50	94.50	95.97	94.15	95.27	94.71	98.16	94.67	**96.39**	94.31
por.rst.cstn	96.76	68.30	80.08	93.18	95.56	**94.35**	90.31	94.44	92.33	92.60	94.12	93.35	90.03
rus.rst.rrt	86.00	64.08	73.44	85.57	86.89	**86.21**	88.19	81.10	84.50	84.93	85.18	85.06	82.30
spa.rst.rststb	88.73	82.17	85.33	92.53	91.96	92.22	92.04	93.04	**92.54**	89.12	94.35	91.66	90.44
spa.rst.sctb	79.34	57.14	66.44	83.44	81.55	82.48	85.39	90.48	**87.86**	92.31	78.57	84.89	80.42
zho.rst.sctb	79.43	66.67	72.49	90.30	77.38	**83.34**	92.48	73.21	81.73	79.89	82.74	81.29	79.71
mean	89.07	71.85	79.27	92.44	90.65	**91.48**	92.24	89.58	90.78	90.74	91.24	90.93	88.12

Table 3: EDU Segmentation Results on Treebanked Data. Disclosure: Systems marked with * were submitted by teams containing organizers and annotators of shared task datasets (see Section 4).

corpus	TMVM			DiscoDisco*			disCut*			SegFormers			mean
(plain)	P	R	F1	P	R	F1	P	R	F1	P	R	F1	
deu.rst.pcc	91.34	86.05	88.62	95.15	92.86	93.94	94.67	96.60	**95.63**	96.81	92.86	94.79	93.25
eng.rst.gum	91.86	64.04	75.46	92.65	92.59	**92.61**	92.76	89.54	91.13	90.38	94.01	92.16	87.84
eng.rst.rstdt	93.37	69.61	79.76	96.80	95.92	**96.35**	93.39	94.50	93.94	94.31	96.16	95.23	91.32
eng.sdrt.stac	83.30	58.37	68.64	91.77	92.06	**91.91**	85.30	87.01	86.14	88.38	87.01	87.69	83.60
eus.rst.ert	84.49	64.05	72.87	92.70	88.38	**90.47**	91.45	83.78	87.45	86.47	90.68	88.52	84.83
fas.rst.prstc	86.77	64.63	74.08	92.95	92.78	**92.86**	93.59	89.40	91.45	94.20	89.70	91.90	87.57
fra.sdrt.annodis	86.33	52.10	64.98	87.95	83.79	85.78	89.90	86.41	88.12	89.67	87.06	**88.34**	81.81
nld.rst.nldt	91.48	82.54	86.78	96.97	92.54	94.69	94.35	93.79	94.07	96.07	94.08	**95.07**	92.65
por.rst.cstn	94.34	65.36	77.22	93.21	95.03	**94.11**	93.36	91.83	92.59	92.60	94.12	93.35	89.32
rus.rst.rrt	84.02	61.29	70.88	87.31	84.24	**85.74**	83.60	84.01	83.80	84.32	84.15	84.23	81.16
spa.rst.rststb	88.86	74.57	81.09	93.30	90.30	**91.76**	92.19	89.78	90.97	90.95	89.57	90.25	88.52
spa.rst.sctb	80.65	59.52	68.49	83.97	77.98	80.86	78.65	89.88	**83.89**	79.78	86.90	83.19	79.11
zho.rst.sctb	83.33	59.52	69.44	84.04	70.00	**76.21**	68.11	75.00	71.39	65.52	79.17	71.70	72.19
mean	87.70	66.28	75.25	91.44	88.34	**89.79**	88.56	88.58	88.51	88.42	89.65	88.96	85.63

Table 4: EDU Segmentation Results on Plain Tokenized Data.

corpus	TMVM			DiscoDisco*			disCut*			SegFormers			mean
(treebanked)	P	R	F1	P	R	F1	P	R	F1	P	R	F1	
eng.pdtb.pdtb	85.98	65.54	74.38	92.93	91.15	**92.02**	93.32	88.67	90.94	89.73	92.61	91.15	87.12
tur.pdtb.tdb	80.00	24.14	37.10	93.71	94.53	**94.11**	90.55	86.93	88.70	90.42	91.17	90.79	77.68
zho.pdtb.cdtb	30.00	0.96	1.86	89.19	85.95	**87.52**	84.43	66.03	74.10	85.05	87.50	86.26	62.44
mean	65.33	30.21	37.78	91.94	90.54	**91.22**	89.43	80.54	84.58	88.40	90.43	89.40	75.75

(plain)	P	R	F1	P	R	F1	P	R	F1	P	R	F1	mean
eng.pdtb.pdtb	81.06	34.37	48.27	94.29	90.92	**92.56**	88.84	92.09	90.43	90.37	91.97	91.16	80.61
tur.pdtb.tdb	73.13	28.86	41.38	91.98	95.22	**93.56**	90.12	88.10	89.10	89.36	91.05	90.20	78.56
zho.pdtb.cdtb	53.33	5.13	9.36	90.27	86.54	**88.35**	77.40	72.44	74.83	85.25	83.33	84.28	64.21
mean	69.17	22.79	33.00	92.18	90.89	**91.49**	85.45	84.21	84.79	88.33	88.78	88.55	74.46

Table 5: Connective Detection Results.

task and the connective detection task; two systems tackled the relation classification task. For teams that submitted multiple systems, we selected the system that achieved the best macro-averaged F-score across datasets as the representative submission. For teams that were not able to obtain all the licensed data, we evaluated submitted systems on the closed LDC datasets for those team and reported the scores to the authors.

EDU Segmentation The main results for EDU segmentation on the test sets are given in Table 3 for treebanked data, and in Table 4 for plain tokenized data. The results indicate improvements across the board for datasets that were represented in the 2019 Shared Task, including new state of the art scores on the benchmark English RST dataset RST-DT (97.09 using gold parses and sentence splits from the system SegFormers, and 96.35 for segmentation from plain text, without sentence boundary information, by the system DisCoDisCo). Improvements are also seen on small datasets, such as Chinese RST, now scoring 83.34 and 76.21 for treebanked / plain text data respectively (both by Dis-

CoDisco), compared to 81.67 and 73.13 in 2019.

The discrepancy between the scores in the two scenarios indicates that gold treebanked data still provides a substantial benefit to EDU segmentation. This may most obviously be the case due to the inclusion of gold sentence splits in the datasets that provide them, which usually coincide with EDU boundaries, though slightly higher scores from approaches using other gold features were also observed (see Section 6 for system analysis).

Connective Detection The main reuslts for connective detection on the test sets are given in Table 5 for both treebanked data and plain tokenized data. As with EDU segmentation, the results show substantial improvements on all datasets compared to 2019, with means climbing from the low 80s to the low 90s. The most notable improvement is on Chinese connective detection, which rises from high 70s to scores around 90, and Turkish, from low 80s to low 90s. The rise in scores for several Transformer-based system scenarios suggests that this may be at least in part a result of improvements in language models for languages other than English.

Relation Classification The main results for the relation classification task are given in Table 6. Since the relation classification task is new, it is difficult to evaluate the quality of the scores obtained in the results. For some datasets, such as PDTB, existing scores have been previously reported on the same underlying data, but generally in different settings, where implicit and explicit relations were scored separately. To make matters worse, most previous work on PDTB uses the older version 2 (Prasad et al., 2008), making scores again completely non-comparable. Previous scores on PDTB-V2 (level 2 relations, the same hierarchical level used for the Shared Task) with explicitly specified connectives have reached scores above 90 for a while (Kido and Aizawa, 2016); more recently, results on PDTB-V3 implicit relation classification have reached an accuracy of 64.83 (Kim et al., 2020). By comparison, we see a best score of 74.44 (DisCoDisCo) on all PDTB-V3 relations (including implicit and explicit), but the task is both easier and harder, since in both cases no connective is specified (for uniformity with other formalisms), but the relation direction is specified in the data (since the Shared Task targets a scenario of labeling unlabeled dependency structures).

corpus	DiscRel	DisCoDisCo*	mean
deu.rst.pcc	35.38	**39.23**	37.31
eng.pdtb.pdtb	50.02	**74.44**	62.23
eng.rst.gum	47.06	**66.76**	56.91
eng.rst.rstdt	55.41	**67.10**	61.26
eng.sdrt.stac	54.11	**65.03**	59.57
eus.rst.ert	44.25	**60.62**	52.44
fas.rst.prstc	**58.95**	52.53	55.74
fra.sdrt.annodis	45.76	**46.40**	46.08
nld.rst.nldt	45.40	**55.21**	50.31
por.rst.cstn	48.53	**64.34**	56.44
rus.rst.rrt	61.34	**66.44**	63.89
spa.rst.rststb	45.07	**54.23**	49.65
spa.rst.sctb	**69.18**	66.04	67.61
tur.pdtb.tdb	48.10	**60.09**	54.10
zho.pdtb.cdtb	**88.65**	86.49	87.57
zho.rst.sctb	**70.44**	64.15	67.30
mean	54.23	61.82	58.02

Table 6: Relation Classification Results.

Results on EDU datasets are equally difficult to compare to previous work due to the focus on full discourse parsing for frameworks like RST, whereas the relation classification task has focused solely on labeling gold graph structures. However, we are encouraged to see best scores above 67 for benchmark datasets such as RST-DT, which beat state-of-the-art discourse dependency parsers' labeled attachment scores (LAS), currently 51.8 (Zhang et al., 2021a); while it is understandable that LAS will always be lower due to the need to predict both attachment and labeling correctly, the Shared Task results indicate that progress on unlabeled attachment (currently 70.2 on RST-DT, ibid.) can lead to substantial gains in labeled accuracy when combined with the approaches tested in this Shared Task.

6 Analysis of Systems

EDU Segmentation and Connective Detection All four systems tackling the segmentation tasks addressed both EDU Segmentation and Connective Detection with a unified architecture, with the partial exception of DisCoDisCo, which varied in using a CRF layer for Connective Detection (in order to model `B-` and `I-` label sequence probabilities), but not for EDU Segmentation, where a CRF layer was found to be harmful.

Of the four systems, the three highest scoring ones relied on a Transformer-based neural sequence labeling approach backed by large, pretrained language models, while the fourth system, TMVM, focused on grammatical features extracted from gold and predicted trees in order to capture clause boundaries across languages. TMVM's submission is also unique in reporting scores when training on each individual dataset and predicting on other datasets using those features, many of which are general across languages. Of the datasets cross-tested by TMVM, training on a different dataset was beneficial for one English case (training on GUM and testing on RST-DT, leading to a 5 point gain from 75 to 80), and the two small Spanish and Chinese datasets (a 3 point gain from 66 to 69 for Spanish when training on the larger Spanish RST STB, and a more modest but surprising 2 point gain from 72 to 74 when training on Basque and testing on Chinese, see Dönicke 2021). The latter two cases are probably owing to the small size of the target corpora. The disCut paper takes a related approach and trains on multiple corpora from the same language or language family, but does not obtain superior results (see Ezzabady et al. 2021), possibly because the single-corpus training results are already so strong.

Among the Transformer-based systems, although DisCoDisCo performs best overall, other systems score highest on particular datasets in different scenarios, with SegFormers attaining a new SOTA score on RST-DT from gold trees (97.09) next to DisCoDisCo's new SOTA score on the same data without gold trees (96.35 in the plain text scenario), and disCut showing impressively strong performance on German (95.61 from gold trees, and an even better 95.63 in the plain text scenario). Overall best scores for EDU Segmentation in the top 3 systems are within a point of each other, but the consistent slight lead of DisCoDisCo may be due to the fact that it was the only segmentation system using per-language transformers and making use of grammatical features, which in the plain text scenario were induced using a SOTA Transformer-based parser and sentence splitter as well.

For Connective Detection, DisCoDisCo's lead becomes slightly larger, about 3 points above SegFormers and almost 7 points above disCut, perhaps due to a combination of features (which give a minor boost of just a few points across datasets in their paper, see Gessler et al. 2021), the use of a CRF layer and the combination of both contextualized and static word embeddings as well as character embeddings, which provided a variety of views on the data and allowed for both fine tuning and fixed generalization in the test set. Choice of language models is also an important factor, and here again disCut and SegFormers rely on multilingual LMs, while DisCoDisCo uses individual per-language models, which may also be a reason for higher scores on Chinese and especially Turkish, which may be less well-represented by multilingual LMs.

Finally we note that in the plain text scenario, all systems except for DisCoDisCo used non-contextualized tools for sentence splitting and/or automatic parsing (SegFormers: CoreNLP; disCut: stanza; TMVM: SpaCy); DisCoDisCo used the tranformer-based sentence splitter from the AMALGUM corpus (Gessler et al., 2020) and DiaParser (Attardi et al., 2021), both with language-specific transformers, with the result that plain text numbers are very close to gold numbers for DisCoDisCo (and in fact insignificantly better for plain Connective Detection: 91.49 on average vs. 91.22 for gold treebanked data). This echoes results from the 2019 task (see Yu et al. 2019) which showed the crucial importance of high quality preprocessing in general, and sentence splitting in particular.

Relation Classification Although both systems tackling the Relation Classification task use word embeddings, their approaches are rather different: while the best system, DisCoDisCo, relies on a similar approach to their segmentation task entry, which encodes each sequence using a transformer, the DiscRel system uses whole sentence embeddings from the Sentence-Transformers library (SBERT, Reimers and Gurevych 2020) to compute Euclidean distance between discourse units, as part of a two-level feature-based Random Forest classifier. Both systems also use the provided discourse relation direction, which is meant to approach the case of labelling an unlabelled discourse dependency graph.

In terms of encoding features, DisCoDisCo uses a sentence pair classifier architecture feeding the underlying transformer embeddings in the form of the BERT classification ([CLS]) token embeddings, while injecting categorical features at two levels: using pseudo tokens, encoded as usual by the transformer, which indicate the relations direction; and using an inserted pseudo token next to the CLS token, which encodes all sequence-level categorical features, such as genre, gold speaker information and more (see Gessler et al. 2021). These features are then read and trained on by the transformer block alongside the word embeddings.

The DiscRel system takes a two level approach to relation classification, using two stacked one-versus-rest Random Forest classifiers, which first attempt to distinguish the coarse class of discourse relation (for example collapsing relations such as EVALUATION, INTERPRETATION, JUSTIFY), and then sub-classify the coarse classes into the final target labels using the second classifier (see Varachkina and Pannach 2021). For large datasets, the first classifier is trained on the train set, while the second is trained using the development data, but for smaller datasets, training data is duplicated along with the development set for the second classifier.

DiscRel's approach performs substantially better for both Chinese datasets, the small Spanish dataset, and Farsi. A commonality in this set is its inclusion of the smallest datasets (the parallel `zho.rst.sctb` and `spa.rst.sctb`), which is perhaps unsurprising given the robustness of tree-based classifiers on small data. However, the gains on the Farsi data, which is not very small, are also substantial, and the system scores over 2 points better than DisCoDisCo on CDTB, suggesting either that SBERT has better embeddings for these languages, or in the case of CDTB, possibly that the small number of target relations (only 9, the smallest relation set) benefits from the stacked classifier approach.

For the remaining 12 datasets, DisCoDisCo scores highest, in many cases by a wide margin of over 10 points above DiscRel (including all English corpora, with +14 on PDTB, +18 on GUM and +12 on RST-DT, and +11 on STAC), leading to a final mean gain of over +7 points. Feature ablations in the DisCoDisCo paper suggest that categorical features confer a minor boost in scores, especially for datasets rich in gold metadata and annotations, but that the primary driver of accuracy is the use of contextualized word embeddings. We also note that, as with segmentation, DisCoDisCo uses language-specific LMs for each dataset, and not always the same LMs as for segmentation, while DiscRel uses one of two multilingual SBERT models for all datasets. For choice of LMs, DisCoDisCo's paper indicates that transformers pretrained with the Next Sentence Prediction task (NSP) are particularly suited to relation classification, i.e. models such as BERT (Devlin et al., 2019), but not the RoBERTa family of models (Liu et al., 2019).

The gaps between the systems given the reproduction and multiple run averages suggest that the two approaches capture some orthogonal information, indicating that incorporating insights from both systems may be worth pursuing: sentence embeddings and Euclidean distance could be incorporated in a neural system, and the features used by DisCoDisCo could be used in a two stage approach such as the one taken by DiscRel.

7 Conclusion

We conducted the second DISRPT shared task for Discourse Relation Parsing and Treebanking across frameworks, resulting in a number of new state of the art scores on benchmark datasets, as well as the publication of a new multilingual benchmark for discourse parsing sub-tasks. With the introduction of the new classification task in 2021, the DISRPT data now covers discourse unit segmentation, connective detection, and relation classification for unit pairs in 16 datasets, coming from 11 languages and containing approx. 3,000,000 tokens.

With the exception of the distinction between Connective Detection and EDU Segmentation datasets, we were able to bring all datasets to a common denominator by relying on a dependency representation of the underlying discourse annotations. Especially in the case of Relation Classification, this means that we can potentially harness the Shared Task data for training and evaluation of discourse relation information using multiple datasets for the same language (where available), and learn from multiple frameworks at the same time. Publishing uniformly evaluated results using a single scorer, input format, and feature set, with a stable reference gold parse for each dataset, we hope to facilitate the conversation and collaboration between researchers coming from different frameworks, such as RST, SDRT, and PDTB.

We are optimistic that the future for computational work on discourse relations is bright, with scores on Segmentation and Connective Detection now looking much higher than in previous years (finally around the low 90s), and Relation Classification slowly catching up, but still offering a substantial challenge with scores in the low 60s. With some luck, we may soon see automatic discourse analysis methods become close to, or even as reliable, as morphosyntactic tagging and parsing have become in recent years. In order to realize that goal, we are certain that we will need new datasets covering previously unexplored languages and genres, as well as in depth analysis of the kinds of discourse relations we should recognize and the challenges in inducing them automatically and reliably across all types of text.

References

Stergos Afantenos, Nicholas Asher, Farah Benamara, Myriam Bras, Cécile Fabre, Mai Ho-dac, Anne Le Draoulec, Philippe Muller, Marie-Paule Péry-Woodley, Laurent Prévot, Josette Rebeyrolles, Ludovic Tanguy, Marianne Vergez-Couret, and Laure Vieu. 2012. An empirical resource for discovering cognitive principles of discourse organisation: the ANNODIS corpus. In *Proceedings of the Eighth International Conference on Language Resources and Evaluation (LREC'12)*, pages 2727–2734, Istanbul, Turkey. European Language Resources Association (ELRA).

Nicholas Asher. 1993. *Reference to abstract objects in discourse*, volume 50. Springer Science & Business Media.

Nicholas Asher, Julie Hunter, Mathieu Morey, Benamara Farah, and Stergos Afantenos. 2016. Discourse structure and dialogue acts in multiparty dialogue: the STAC corpus. In *Proceedings of the Tenth International Conference on Language Resources and Evaluation (LREC'16)*, pages 2721–2727, Portorož, Slovenia. European Language Resources Association (ELRA).

Giuseppe Attardi, Daniele Sartiano, and Maria Simi. 2021. Biaffine dependency and semantic graph parsing for EnhancedUniversal dependencies. In *Proceedings of the 17th International Conference on Parsing Technologies and the IWPT 2021 Shared Task on Parsing into Enhanced Universal Dependencies (IWPT 2021)*, pages 184–188, Online. Association for Computational Linguistics.

Chloé Braud, Maximin Coavoux, and Anders Søgaard. 2017. Cross-lingual RST discourse parsing. In *Proceedings of the 15th Conference of the European Chapter of the Association for Computational Linguistics: Volume 1, Long Papers*, pages 292–304, Valencia, Spain. Association for Computational Linguistics.

Shuyuan Cao, Iria da Cunha, and Mikel Iruskieta. 2018. The RST Spanish-Chinese treebank. In *Proceedings of the Joint Workshop on Linguistic Annotation, Multiword Expressions and Constructions (LAW-MWE-CxG-2018)*, pages 156–166, Santa Fe, New Mexico, USA. Association for Computational Linguistics.

Paula Christina Figueira Cardoso, Erick Galani Maziero, Maria Lucía del Rosario Castro Jorge, M. Eloize, R. Kibar Aji Seno, Ariani Di Felippo, Lucia Helena Machado Rino, Maria das Graças Volpe Nunes, and Thiago Alexandre Salgueiro Pardo. 2011. CSTNews - a discourse-annotated corpus for single and multi-document summarization of news texts in Brazilian Portuguese. In *Proceedings of the 3rd RST Brazilian Meeting*, pages 88–105, Cuiabá, Brazil.

Lynn Carlson, Daniel Marcu, and Mary Ellen Okurovsky. 2001. Building a discourse-tagged corpus in the framework of Rhetorical Structure Theory. In *Proceedings of the Second SIGdial Workshop on Discourse and Dialogue*.

Iria da Cunha, Juan-Manuel Torres-Moreno, and Gerardo Sierra. 2011. On the development of the RST Spanish treebank. In *Proceedings of the 5th Linguistic Annotation Workshop*, pages 1–10, Portland, Oregon, USA. Association for Computational Linguistics.

Vera Demberg, Fatemeh Torabi Asr, and Merel Scholman. 2019. How consistent are our discourse annotations? Insights from mapping RST-DT and PDTB annotations. *Dialogue & Discourse*, 10(1):87—135.

Jacob Devlin, Ming-Wei Chang, Kenton Lee, and Kristina Toutanova. 2019. BERT: Pre-training of deep bidirectional transformers for language understanding. In *Proceedings of the 2019 Conference of the North American Chapter of the Association for Computational Linguistics: Human Language Technologies, Volume 1 (Long and Short Papers)*, pages 4171–4186, Minneapolis, Minnesota. Association for Computational Linguistics.

Tillmann Dönicke. 2021. Delexicalised Multilingual Discourse Segmentation for DISRPT 2021 and Tense, Mood, Voice and Modality Tagging for 11 Languages. In *Proceedings of Discourse Relation Parsing and Treebanking 2021 (DISRPT 2021)*, Punta Cana, Dominican Republic.

Carla Parra Escartín, Teresa Lynn, J. Moorkens, and Jane Dunne. 2021. Towards transparency in NLP shared tasks. *ArXiv*, abs/2105.05020.

Morteza Kamaladdini Ezzabady, Philippe Muller, and Chloé Braud. 2021. Multi-lingual Discourse Segmentation and Connective Identification: MELODI at DISRPT2021. In *Proceedings of Discourse Relation Parsing and Treebanking 2021 (DISRPT 2021)*, Punta Cana, Dominican Republic.

Luke Gessler, Shabnam Behzad, Yang Janet Liu, Siyao Peng, Yilun Zhu, and Amir Zeldes. 2021. DisCoDisCo at the DISRPT2021 Shared Task: A System for Discourse Segmentation, Classification, and Connective Detection. In *Proceedings of Discourse Relation Parsing and Treebanking 2021 (DISRPT 2021)*, Punta Cana, Dominican Republic.

Luke Gessler, Siyao Peng, Yang Liu, Yilun Zhu, Shabnam Behzad, and Amir Zeldes. 2020. AMALGUM – a free, balanced, multilayer English web corpus. In *Proceedings of the 12th Language Resources and Evaluation Conference*, pages 5267–5275, Marseille, France. European Language Resources Association.

Grigorii Guz and Giuseppe Carenini. 2020. Coreference for discourse parsing: A neural approach. In *Proceedings of the First Workshop on Computational Approaches to Discourse*, pages 160–167, Online. Association for Computational Linguistics.

Mikel Iruskieta, María Jesús Aranzabe, Arantza Diaz de Ilarraza, Itziar Gonzalez-Dios, Mikel Lersundi, and Oier Lopez de Lacalle. 2013. The RST Basque TreeBank: An online search interface to check rhetorical relations. In *4th Workshop on RST and Discourse Studies*, pages 40–49, Fortaleza, Brasil.

Yusuke Kido and Akiko Aizawa. 2016. Discourse relation sense classification with two-step classifiers. In *Proceedings of the CoNLL-16 shared task*, pages 129–135, Berlin, Germany. Association for Computational Linguistics.

Najoung Kim, Song Feng, Chulaka Gunasekara, and Luis Lastras. 2020. Implicit discourse relation classification: We need to talk about evaluation. In *Proceedings of the 58th Annual Meeting of the Association for Computational Linguistics*, pages 5404–5414, Online. Association for Computational Linguistics.

Murathan Kurfali. 2020. Labeling explicit discourse relations using pre-trained language models. In *Text, Speech, and Dialogue. TSD 2020*, pages 79–86, Brno, Czech Republic. Springer.

Qi Li, Tianshi Li, and Baobao Chang. 2016. Discourse parsing with attention-based hierarchical neural networks. In *Proceedings of the 2016 Conference on Empirical Methods in Natural Language Processing*, pages 362–371, Austin, Texas. Association for Computational Linguistics.

Xin Liu, Jiefu Ou, Yangqiu Song, and Xin Jiang. 2020. On the importance of word and sentence representation learning in implicit discourse relation classification. In *Proceedings of the Twenty-Ninth International Joint Conference on Artificial Intelligence, IJCAI-20*, pages 3830–3836. International Joint Conferences on Artificial Intelligence Organization. Main track.

Yinhan Liu, Myle Ott, Naman Goyal, Jingfei Du, Mandar Joshi, Danqi Chen, Omer Levy, M. Lewis, Luke Zettlemoyer, and Veselin Stoyanov. 2019. RoBERTa: A Robustly Optimized BERT Pretraining Approach. *ArXiv*, abs/1907.11692.

William C. Mann and Sandra A. Thompson. 1988. Rhetorical Structure Theory: Toward a functional theory of text organization. *Text*, 8(3):243–281.

Mathieu Morey, Philippe Muller, and Nicholas Asher. 2018. A dependency perspective on RST discourse parsing and evaluation. *Computational Linguistics*, 44(2):197–235.

Allen Nie, Erin Bennett, and Noah Goodman. 2019. DisSent: Learning sentence representations from explicit discourse relations. In *Proceedings of the 57th Annual Meeting of the Association for Computational Linguistics*, pages 4497–4510, Florence, Italy. Association for Computational Linguistics.

Jérémy Perret, Stergos Afantenos, Nicholas Asher, and Mathieu Morey. 2016. Integer linear programming for discourse parsing. In *Proceedings of the 2016 Conference of the North American Chapter of the Association for Computational Linguistics: Human Language Technologies*, pages 99–109, San Diego, California. Association for Computational Linguistics.

Rashmi Prasad, Nikhil Dinesh, Alan Lee, Eleni Miltsakaki, Livio Robaldo, Aravind Joshi, and Bonnie Webber. 2008. The Penn Discourse TreeBank 2.0. In *Proceedings of the Sixth International Conference on Language Resources and Evaluation (LREC'08)*, Marrakech, Morocco. European Language Resources Association (ELRA).

Rashmi Prasad, Bonnie Webber, and Aravind Joshi. 2014. Reflections on the Penn Discourse TreeBank, comparable corpora, and complementary annotation. *Computational Linguistics*, 40(4):921–950.

Gisela Redeker, Ildikó Berzlánovich, Nynke van der Vliet, Gosse Bouma, and Markus Egg. 2012. Multi-layer discourse annotation of a Dutch text corpus. In *Proceedings of the Eighth International Conference on Language Resources and Evaluation (LREC'12)*, pages 2820–2825, Istanbul, Turkey. European Language Resources Association (ELRA).

Nils Reimers and Iryna Gurevych. 2020. Making monolingual sentence embeddings multilingual using knowledge distillation. In *Proceedings of the 2020 Conference on Empirical Methods in Natural Language Processing (EMNLP)*, pages 4512–4525, Online. Association for Computational Linguistics.

Sara Shahmohammadi, Hadi Veisi, and Ali Darzi. 2021. Persian Rhetorical Structure Theory. *arXiv preprint arXiv:2106.13833*.

Manfred Stede and Arne Neumann. 2014. Potsdam commentary corpus 2.0: Annotation for discourse research. In *Proceedings of the Ninth International Conference on Language Resources and Evaluation (LREC'14)*, pages 925–929, Reykjavik, Iceland. European Language Resources Association (ELRA).

Svetlana Toldova, Dina Pisarevskaya, Margarita Ananyeva, Maria Kobozeva, Alexander Nasedkin, Sofia Nikiforova, Irina Pavlova, and Alexey Shelepov. 2017. Rhetorical relations markers in Russian RST treebank. In *Proceedings of the 6th Workshop on Recent Advances in RST and Related Formalisms*, pages 29–33, Santiago de Compostela, Spain. Association for Computational Linguistics.

Hanna Varachkina and Franziska Pannach. 2021. A Unified Approach to Discourse Relation Classification in nine Languages. In *Proceedings of Discourse Relation Parsing and Treebanking 2021 (DISRPT 2021)*, Punta Cana, Dominican Republic.

Jianxiang Wang and Man Lan. 2015. A refined end-to-end discourse parser. In *Proceedings of the Nine-*

teenth Conference on Computational Natural Language Learning - Shared Task, pages 17–24, Beijing, China. Association for Computational Linguistics.

Jianxiang Wang and Man Lan. 2016. Two end-to-end shallow discourse parsers for English and Chinese in CoNLL-2016 shared task. In *Proceedings of the CoNLL-16 shared task*, pages 33–40, Berlin, Germany. Association for Computational Linguistics.

Yue Yu, Yilun Zhu, Yang Liu, Yan Liu, Siyao Peng, Mackenzie Gong, and Amir Zeldes. 2019. GumDrop at the DISRPT2019 shared task: A model stacking approach to discourse unit segmentation and connective detection. In *Proceedings of Discourse Relation Treebanking and Parsing (DISRPT 2019)*, pages 133–143, Minneapolis, MN.

Amir Zeldes. 2017. The GUM corpus: Creating multilayer resources in the classroom. *Language Resources and Evaluation*, 51(3):581–612.

Amir Zeldes, Debopam Das, Erick Galani Maziero, Juliano Antonio, and Mikel Iruskieta. 2019. The DISRPT 2019 shared task on elementary discourse unit segmentation and connective detection. In *Proceedings of the Workshop on Discourse Relation Parsing and Treebanking 2019*, pages 97–104, Minneapolis, MN. Association for Computational Linguistics.

Deniz Zeyrek and Murathan Kurfalı. 2017. TDB 1.1: Extensions on Turkish discourse bank. In *Proceedings of the 11th Linguistic Annotation Workshop*, pages 76–81, Valencia, Spain. Association for Computational Linguistics.

Deniz Zeyrek and Bonnie Webber. 2008. A discourse resource for Turkish: Annotating discourse connectives in the METU corpus. In *Proceedings of the 6th Workshop on Asian Language Resources*.

Liwen Zhang, Ge Wang, Wenjuan Han, and Kewei Tu. 2021a. Adapting unsupervised syntactic parsing methodology for discourse dependency parsing. In *Proceedings of the 59th Annual Meeting of the Association for Computational Linguistics and the 11th International Joint Conference on Natural Language Processing (Volume 1: Long Papers)*, pages 5782–5794, Online. Association for Computational Linguistics.

Longyin Zhang, Fang Kong, and Guodong Zhou. 2021b. Adversarial learning for discourse rhetorical structure parsing. In *Proceedings of the 59th Annual Meeting of the Association for Computational Linguistics and the 11th International Joint Conference on Natural Language Processing (Volume 1: Long Papers)*, pages 3946–3957, Online. Association for Computational Linguistics.

Yuping Zhou, Jill Lu, Jennifer Zhang, and Nianwen Xue. 2014. Chinese Discourse Treebank 0.5 LDC2014T21.

A Transformer Based Approach towards Identification of Discourse Unit Segments and Connectives

Sahil Bakshi and **Dipti Misra Sharma**

Language Technologies Research Center (LTRC)
International Institute of Information Technology, Hyderabad, India

sahil.bakshi@research.iiit.ac.in, dipti@iiit.ac.in

Abstract

Discourse parsing, which involves understanding the structure, information flow, and modeling the coherence of a given text, is an important task in natural language processing. It forms the basis of several natural language processing tasks such as question-answering, text summarization, and sentiment analysis. Discourse unit segmentation is one of the fundamental tasks in discourse parsing and refers to identifying the elementary units of text that combine to form a coherent text. In this paper, we present a transformer based approach towards the automated identification of discourse unit segments and connectives. Early approaches towards segmentation relied on rule-based systems using POS tags and other syntactic information to identify discourse segments. Recently, transformer based neural systems have shown promising results in this domain. Our system, SegFormers, employs this transformer based approach to perform multilingual discourse segmentation and connective identification across 16 datasets encompassing 11 languages and 3 different annotation frameworks. We evaluate the system based on F1 scores for both tasks, with the best system reporting the highest F1 score of 97.02% for the treebanked English RST-DT dataset.

1 Introduction

Discourse is defined as a coherent, structured group of sentences (Jurafsky and Martin, 2009). Discourse parsing enables the creation of models for further downstream natural language processing tasks such as question-answering, text summarization, information retrieval and extraction, sentiment analysis, and argument mining. Discourse segmentation is a fundamental task in discourse parsing, which involves identifying the minimal chunks of text that combine to form a coherent discourse. In the Rhetorical Structure Theory (RST) (Mann and Thompson, 1988) framework, these basic chunks of texts are known as Elementary Discourse Units (EDUs). These EDUs are linked together by discourse relations which may be explicit (when explicitly marked in the text by a discourse connective) or implicit. Segmentation refers to the task of identifying these EDUs. There have been several approaches towards the identification of these discourse segments. Another popular framework is the Segmented Discourse Representation Theory (SDRT) (Asher and Lascarides, 2003). Both these frameworks segment the text into non-overlapping spans covering entire documents. The discourse segmentation task, in this case, corresponds to identifying the starting point of each discourse unit. In 2008, the Penn Discourse TreeBank (PDTB) (Prasad et al., 2008) was released with a corpus of over 1 million words. The unit identification task for this framework corresponds to identifying the spans of discourse connectives that explicitly identify the existence of a discourse relation.

The task of EDU segmentation has been widely researched in the past due to its importance as a building block for further downstream natural language processing tasks. Most of the previous research concerning EDU segmentation has relied on the information obtained from syntactic elements of the text such as syntactic parse trees (Tofiloski et al., 2009 ; Le Thanh et al., 2004). However, recent works have explored the task of segmentation using systems based on neural networks using the BiLSTM - CRF framework (Wang et al., 2018) or the attention mechanism (Li et al., 2016). Another important factor in all the previous works has been the presence/absence of gold sentence boundaries (Ji and Eisenstein, 2014 ; Feng and Hirst, 2014) in the data.

The DISRPT 2021 Shared Task introduces the second iteration of a cross-formalism shared task on discourse unit segmentation and connective detection, and the first iteration of a cross-formalism discourse relation classification task. The organizers provided 16 datasets in the RST (Mann and

Proceedings of the 2nd Shared Task on Discourse Relation Parsing and Treebanking (DISRPT 2021), pages 13–21
November 11, 2021.

Thompson, 1988), SDRT (Asher and Lascarides, 2003) and PDTB (Prasad et al., 2008) formalisms with each dataset consisting of a training, development, and test set. The data has been provided in two formats - one is the treebanked format which provides the gold syntax and the other is the plain tokenized data without the gold syntax. This encourages the system design to be able to adapt and deal with data when the gold syntax is not provided.

In this paper, we describe our approach towards the discourse unit segmentation and connective detection tasks using a model based on the transformers architecture (Devlin et al., 2018) with a classification layer on top to provide the outputs. We report scores for discourse segmentation and connective identification on both settings - data with gold sentence boundaries as well as document level boundaries. Our best results improve the previous task iterations' (Zeldes et al., 2019) best results on 15 out of the 16 available datasets.

2 Related Work

Early work in the domain for discourse parsing involved rule-based models which used syntactic information for the prediction of discourse segments and connectives (Tofiloski et al., 2009). Le Thanh et al. (2004) used syntactic information and cue phrases to segment sentences into EDUs and integrated constraints about textual adjacency and textual organization in a beam search for text level segmentation. Soricut and Marcu (2003) used probabilistic models for EDU identification on the RST-DT corpus (Carlson et al., 2003). Building on this, Subba and Di Eugenio (2007) developed a neural network model for discourse segmentation using the same RST-DT dataset (Carlson et al., 2003). A token based classifier was introduced by Sporleder and Lapata (2005) which used POS tags, syntactic chunks, and clause information as features for the segmentation task.

Fisher and Roark (2007) investigated the approach towards segmentation using sentence level syntactic parse trees on the RST-DT corpus. On a similar note, Jain and Sharma (2016) introduced a hybrid pipeline for discourse connective and argument identification in Hindi using sub-tree extraction and linear tagging approaches. The data for this system was obtained from the Hindi Discourse Relation Bank (HDRB) (Oza et al., 2009). The importance of dependency information was investigated by Braud et al. (2017b) by introducing a segmentation model that only relies on part-of-speech information. Pitler and Nenkova (2009) proposed a method of using syntactic features for the identification of discourse connectives and the disambiguation of the connective in terms of its usage and the relation they mark.

Recent studies have been moving towards machine learning based approaches with most involving the use of sequential neural network models. Li et al. (2018) used a bidirectional recurrent neural network along with a pointer network to select text boundaries in the input sequence. An end-to-end neural segmenter was proposed by Wang et al. (2018) based on the BiLSTM-CRF framework. Their system reported new state-of-the-art performance on the RST-DT corpus (Carlson et al., 2003) with an F1 score of 94.3%. Lukasik et al. (2020) investigate a transformers based approach towards document and discourse level segmentation with the RST-DT corpus being used for discourse segmentation and the Wiki-727K dataset (Koshorek et al., 2018) for document segmentation experiments. Braud et al. (2017a) introduced the first multilingual segmenter across 5 languages and 3 non-newswire English domains using language independent tools.

Segmenters have also been developed for other languages with Lüngen et al. (2006) proposing a discourse segmenter for German, Iruskieta and Zapirain (2015) for Basque, Afantenos et al. (2010) for French, van der Vliet (2010) for Dutch, Pardo and Nunes (2008) for Brazilian Portuguese, Da Cunha et al. (2012) for Spanish and Yang and Li (2018) for Chinese.

3 Datasets

In this section, we describe the datasets provided by the organizers of the CODI-DISRPT2021: Discourse Relation Parsing and Treebanking Shared Task at EMNLP 2021[1]. The data provided consists of 16 datasets comprising of 11 languages (German, English, Basque, Persian, French, Dutch, Portuguese, Russian, Spanish, Turkish, and Mandarin Chinese). This is the first iteration of the Persian RST corpus (Shahmohammadi et al., 2021) being included for the task of discourse segmentation. The Chinese PDTB dataset (Zhou and Xue, 2015) is not available freely. Hence, the organizers provided the scores on this dataset after running the

[1]https://sites.google.com/georgetown.edu/disrpt2021/

model on the CDTB dataset during the evaluation phase.

3.1 Annotation frameworks

The data for discourse unit segmentation and connective detection tasks has been provided in the RST, SDRT, and PDTB formalisms. The tasks differ across different formalisms. In the RST and SDRT framework, the text has been segmented into non-overlapping spans covering each entire documents. The corresponding task, in this case, is finding the starting point of each discourse unit. In the PDTB framework, the segmentation task corresponds to identifying the spans of discourse connectives that explicitly identify the presence of a discourse relation.

Out of the 16 datasets, 3 corpora follow the PDTB framework (English, Turkish, and Mandarin Chinese), 2 are represented by the SDRT framework (English and French), and 11 datasets follow the RST framework. The diversity across the datasets with respect to the frameworks encourages the design of flexible systems capable of dealing with multiple formalisms.

3.2 Languages

The organizers have provided data for 11 languages. There are 4 datasets for the English language (Prasad et al., 2008 ; Zeldes, 2017 ; Carlson et al., 2003 ; Asher et al., 2016), 2 for Spanish (Da Cunha et al., 2011 ; Cao et al., 2018), 2 for Mandarin Chinese (Zhou and Xue, 2015 ; Cao et al., 2018) and 1 each for German (Stede and Neumann, 2014), Basque (Iruskieta et al., 2013 ; Aranzabe et al., 2015), Persian (Shahmohammadi et al., 2021), French (Péry-Woodley et al., 2011), Dutch (Redeker et al., 2012), Portuguese (Cardoso et al., 2011), Russian (Toldova et al., 2017), and Turkish (Zeyrek and Kurfalı, 2017).

The Persian RST corpus was added as a surprise language dataset at the release of the test data.

3.3 Data statistics

We present a comprehensive overview of the datasets provided by the organizers in Table 1. For the tasks of discourse unit segmentation and connective identification, each dataset has a training, development, and test set available in 2 file formats, as treebanked .conllu files which have a gold dependency parse and plain .tok files which contain plain tokens. The labels in the RST and SDRT framework denote the beginning of a discourse segment. The PDTB framework consists of labels that mark the entire span of discourse connectives that explicitly identify the existence of a discourse relation.

The English PDTB corpus is the largest in the given datasets with 1,061,229 training tokens and 1,156,657 total tokens in the dataset. The Chinese section of the RST Spanish - Chinese treebank is the smallest corpus with 9,655 training tokens and a total of 15,496 tokens. These variations in the dataset size, frameworks, and languages render the task challenging. You can find the datasets at the official DISRPT 2021 GitHub repository here[2].

4 System Overview

In this section, we present our approach towards the tasks of discourse unit segmentation and connective identification. We establish a baseline using a bidirectional LSTM classifier and propose a final system using the transformers architecture (Devlin et al., 2018) with a classification layer on top.

4.1 Bidirectional LSTM

Bidirectional LSTMs are basically an extension to the LSTM model (Hochreiter and Schmidhuber, 1997) and can be thought of as joining two LSTMs together. This architecture allows the model to read input sequences in both forward and backward directions, which results in an effective capture of context, which helps in improving model performance for classification tasks.

As a baseline, we propose a PyTorch[3] implementation of a simple bidirectional LSTM which encodes input tokens using word embeddings and has a single linear layer for the segmentation task. The model takes in an input sequence of tokens along with the corresponding sequence of labels, converts them into word vectors, and passes them to the bidirectional LSTM. The final linear layer takes the hidden states as input from the bidirectional LSTM and outputs the final labels.

4.2 SegFormers

Recent studies have shown promising results with neural approaches towards NLP tasks. Transformer (Vaswani et al., 2017) based architectures like BERT (Devlin et al., 2018) achieved state-of-the-art scores on several natural language processing tasks. Following this, Devlin et al. (2018) proposed

[2] `https://github.com/disrpt/sharedtask2021`

[3] `https://pytorch.org/`

Corpus	Language	Framework	Train Tokens	Train Sent.	Train Docs.
deu.rst.pcc	German	RST	26,831	1,773	142
eng.rst.gum	English	RST	116,557	6,346	128
eng.rst.rstdt	English	RST	166,854	6,672	309
eus.rst.ert	Basque	RST	30,690	1,599	116
fas.rst.prstc	Persian	RST	52,497	1,713	120
nld.rst.nldt	Dutch	RST	17,562	1,156	56
por.rst.cstn	Portuguese	RST	52,177	1,825	114
rus.rst.rrt	Russian	RST	390,375	18,932	272
spa.rst.rststb	Spanish	RST	43,055	1,548	203
spa.rst.sctb	Spanish	RST	10,253	326	32
zho.rst.sctb	Chinese	RST	9,655	361	32
eng.sdrt.stac	English	SDRT	41,060	8,754	33
fra.sdrt.annodis	French	SDRT	22,515	1,020	64
eng.pdtb.pdtb	English	PDTB	1,061,229	44,563	1,992
tur.pdtb.tdb	Turkish	PDTB	398,515	24,960	159
zho.pdtb.cdtb	Chinese	PDTB	52,061	2,049	125

Table 1: Datasets for the segmentation tasks

a multilingual BERT model[4] pretrained on 104 languages in a self supervised fashion. We adopt the aforementioned model and modify it for the segmentation and connective detection tasks.

Previous approaches towards EDU segmentation adopt a sequence classification approach. Wang et al. (2018) employed a self attention mechanism (Vaswani et al., 2017) restricting the attention area for the model to a neighborhood of fixed size which would prevent the unnecessary tokens from misleading the model. Building upon this, we present the task of segmentation as a token classification problem to the multilingual BERT model. This enables the architecture to learn and gain information from each individual token and spares it from committing errors due to unnecessary tokens. The multilingual BERT model has been trained on a huge corpus of multilingual data which makes it capable of being fine tuned to handle downstream tasks such as token classification even when the available training dataset is not very large.

Our system, SegFormers, takes sequences of tokens and corresponding labels as input which are then fed into a tokenizer. The WordPiece tokenizer converts the words into tokens to be fed into the model. One issue that arises, in this case, is the problem of out of vocabulary words. In such cases, the tokenizer splits the input word into subtokens which are present in the tokenizer vocabulary. This creates a mismatch between the number of input tokens and labels. We handle this issue by modifying the label tokenization process to match the output length. The tokenizer returns an offset mapping for each split word, according to which we then modify the label encodings. This ensures efficiency in the training process. We obtain the segmentation outputs by adding a linear layer that takes the outputs from the hidden states and converts them into the segmentation boundary labels.

This system is suited for the treebanked (.conllu files) data since the lengths of the input sequences stay below the threshold of 512 tokens. However, in the case of plain tokenized documents (.tok files), the input sequences are entire documents whose length goes beyond the 512 token limit. We work around this by adopting the approach of Muller et al. (2019) and using the StanfordNLP sentence splitter[5] for splitting the input document sequences into sentences.

Figure 1 illustrates the basic architecture and data flow in our proposed system. The results obtained from our system indicate that fine-tuning the multilingual BERT model by considering discourse unit segmentation as a token classification task instead of a sequence labeling task leads to better model performance.

[4] `https://github.com/google-research/bert`

[5] `https://stanfordnlp.github.io/CoreNLP/ssplit.html`

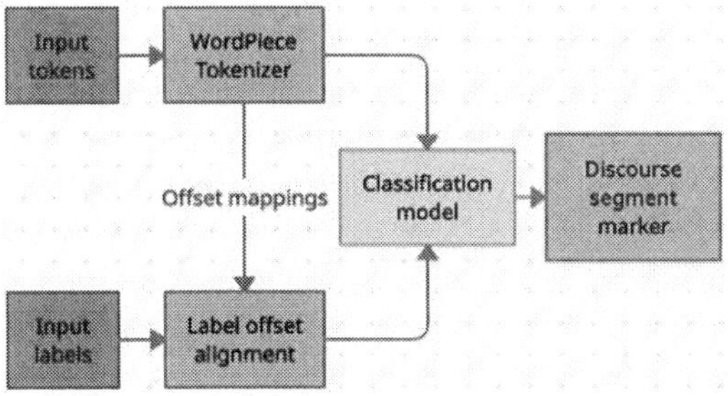

Figure 1: System architecture and data flow

5 Experimental Settings

For the bidirectional LSTM model, we used 300 dimensional randomly initialized word embeddings to encode the input tokens and pass it to a hidden layer with 100 dimensions and a dropout rate of 0.5. We used the Adam optimizer to update the model weights with a learning rate of 1e-3 and a batch size of 1 for training. We used the negative log-likelihood loss and trained the model for 5 epochs to obtain the optimal results.

For our system, we used HuggingFace's[6] PyTorch implementation of the multilingual BERT model. We fine tuned the model to work with the discourse unit segmentation task and present the optimal model settings for the same. We used a batch size of 8 for the training of the model. We experimented with various preprocessing and training parameters, changing the padding and truncation length, tweaking the weight update rate, and changing the number of training epochs. We found that the best results were obtained when the input sequences in the batch were padded to the length of the longest sequence in that given batch. We used the AdamW optimizer with a learning rate of 1e-5 and trained for 5 epochs to obtain the best F1 scores.

6 Results

Our system, SegFormers, improves the best scores of the previous iteration's results for 15 out of the 16 provided datasets for the discourse unit segmentation and the connective identification tasks. In this section, we present the detailed results of all our systems. The final precision, recall and F1 scores have been provided by the organizers by averaging the scores obtained over 5 runs.

[6]https://huggingface.co/

Corpus	P	R	F1
deu.rst.pcc	93.71	96.26	94.97
eng.rst.gum	91.47	95.67	93.52
eng.rst.rstdt	96.15	98.04	**97.09**
eng.sdrt.stac	96.73	95.67	96.20
eus.rst.ert	87.23	88.65	87.94
fas.rst.prstc	90.53	94.18	92.32
fra.sdrt.annodis	86.76	88.03	87.39
nld.rst.nldt	98.16	94.67	96.39
por.rst.cstn	92.60	94.12	93.35
rus.rst.rrt	84.93	85.18	85.06
spa.rst.rststb	89.12	94.35	91.66
spa.rst.sctb	92.31	78.57	84.89
zho.rst.sctb	79.89	82.74	81.29
mean	**90.74**	**91.24**	**90.93**

Table 2: SegFormers scores for the EDU segmentation task on the treebanked (.conllu files) data. The best score has been marked in bold. The model performs the best on the English RST-DT dataset with an F1 score of 97.09%.

6.1 Bidirectional LSTM

We report the baseline accuracy, precision, recall, and F1 scores on the development and test sets for the 15 available datasets based on the outputs obtained from the bidirectional LSTM model in Table 3. The bidirectional LSTM model gives largely decent scores on most of the datasets, with the lowest being 65.979% F1 score for the segmentation task on the zho.rst.sctb dataset and 66.292% F1 score for the connective identification task on the tur.pdtb.tdb dataset. For the segmentation task, the model attains its best performance on the nld.rst.nldt dataset with an F1 score of 85.362% and similarly, 78.629% F1 score on the eng.pdtb.pdtb dataset for connective identification task. The low F1 scores on the Chinese RST dataset can be attributed to the small training dataset size with only 32 documents consisting of 9,655 tokens available for training. On many datasets, the precision scores are quite higher than the recall (Basque dataset - 95% precision and 61% recall, Russian dataset - 84% precision and 60% recall), indicating that the model is primarily aiming for the generic discourse unit boundary detection at the beginning of the discourse segments.

6.2 SegFormers

We report the discourse segmentation results from our multilingual transformers based model, Seg-

	Development Set				Test Set			
Corpus	**Acc**	**P**	**R**	**F1**	**Acc**	**P**	**R**	**F1**
deu.rst.pcc	97.239	89.166	77.818	83.106	97.190	90.763	76.870	83.241
eng.pdtb.pdtb	98.873	81.446	76.117	78.692	98.882	78.870	76.578	77.707
eng.rst.gum	95.226	80.000	83.399	81.664	95.247	78.860	84.227	81.455
eng.rst.rstdt	96.614	82.961	84.808	83.874	96.436	81.785	86.317	83.990
eng.sdrt.stac	90.878	79.049	85.008	81.920	90.835	79.246	82.934	81.048
eus.rst.ert	95.927	93.821	60.561	73.608	96.112	95.974	61.216	74.752
fas.rst.prstc	97.534	90.380	78.298	83.906	97.272	90.500	78.208	83.907
fra.sdrt.annodis	96.120	91.666	71.223	80.161	95.678	90.890	70.806	79.601
nld.rst.nldt	97.488	90.522	80.758	85.362	97.382	91.525	79.881	**85.308**
por.rst.cstn	95.974	75.698	86.031	80.534	96.749	74.863	89.542	81.547
rus.rst.rrt	95.892	84.981	60.769	70.864	95.734	84.391	60.262	70.314
spa.rst.rststb	98.119	84.367	81.145	82.725	97.756	80.616	79.565	80.087
spa.rst.sctb	97.834	79.761	65.048	71.657	97.771	81.679	63.690	71.571
tur.pdtb.tdb	98.741	63.533	70.037	66.627	98.693	62.632	70.405	66.292
zho.rst.sctb	97.040	68.000	66.019	66.995	97.232	78.048	57.142	65.979

Table 3: Results for the baseline bidirectional LSTM model on the 15 available datasets for the tasks of EDU segmentation and connective detection. The model performs the best on the Dutch RST dataset with an F1 score of 85.308%.

Formers, in Tables 2 and 4. Our system returns high F1 scores across all 16 provided datasets and manages to improve the previous best scores on all except the French ANNODIS corpus in the treebanked scenario. We also report better scores for 14 out of the 16 provided datasets in the plain document level (.tok files) setting with only the French ANNODIS corpus and the Chinese section of the RST Spanish-Chinese Treebank, yielding scores lower than the previous best results.

We also report the first ever scores for the Persian RST corpus (Shahmohammadi et al., 2021) with our system returning the best F1 score of 92.32% in the treebanked scenario with the gold syntax and the best F1 score of 91.90% on the plain tokenized documents.

We observe significant improvements compared to the previous iteration results on the Basque dataset (F1 score of 88.52% compared to the previous best F1 score of 84.06%) with the plain tokenized documents. To the best of our knowledge, we also report state-of-the-art performance so far for discourse unit segmentation on the English RST-DT dataset with an F1 score of 97.09% on the test dataset with the gold syntax.

With respect to the task of connective identification on the datasets with the PDTB framework, we could only obtain results on the English and Turkish PDTB datasets since the Chinese CDTB

Corpus	**P**	**R**	**F1**
deu.rst.pcc	96.81	92.86	94.79
eng.rst.gum	90.38	94.01	92.16
eng.rst.rstdt	94.31	96.16	**95.23**
eng.sdrt.stac	88.38	87.01	87.69
eus.rst.ert	86.47	90.68	88.52
fas.rst.prstc	94.20	89.70	91.90
fra.sdrt.annodis	89.67	87.06	88.34
nld.rst.nldt	96.07	94.08	95.07
por.rst.cstn	92.60	94.12	93.35
rus.rst.rrt	84.32	84.15	84.23
spa.rst.rststb	90.95	89.57	90.25
spa.rst.sctb	79.78	86.90	83.19
zho.rst.sctb	65.52	79.17	71.70
mean	**88.42**	**89.65**	**88.96**

Table 4: SegFormers scores for the EDU segmentation task on the plain tokenized (.tok files) data. The best score has been marked in bold. The model performs the best on the English RST-DT corpus with an F1 score of 95.23%.

	Treebanked (.conllu) data			Plain tokenized (.tok) data		
Corpus	**P**	**R**	**F1**	**P**	**R**	**F1**
eng.pdtb.pdtb	89.72	92.61	91.14	90.37	91.96	**91.16**
tur.pdtb.tdb	90.42	91.16	**90.79**	89.36	91.04	90.19
zho.pdtb.cdtb	85.04	87.50	**86.25**	85.24	83.33	84.27
mean	**88.39**	**90.42**	**89.39**	**88.32**	**88.78**	**88.54**

Table 5: Final SegFormers scores for the connective detection task on the PDTB framework datasets. The best scores for each dataset have been marked in bold. The model performs the best on the English PDTB dataset with an F1 score of 91.16%.

dataset was not freely available. The organizers provided the scores on the Chinese CDTB dataset after the evaluation phase. We report the F1 scores for our model on these datasets in Table 5 for the treebanked and plain scenario.

Comparing the results of the model on the treebanked data with the results on the plain tokenized documents, we can see that the performance of the model is consistently better on the treebanked datasets, with the Chinese section of the RST Spanish-Chinese Treebank showing the most significant drop in F1 scores (81.29% to 71.70%). There are a couple of exceptions, with the model giving better scores for the Basque and Spanish RST datasets. However, in general, we can conclude that the presence of gold sentence boundaries helps the system perform better compared to the datasets with predicted sentence boundary markers.

7 Conclusion and Future Work

In this paper, we looked at the topic of discourse segmentation and its importance in the development of robust models for further downstream natural language processing tasks. We report our approach towards building a system for the EDU segmentation and connective identification tasks across 16 datasets consisting of 11 languages and 3 frameworks. We present a multilingual system leveraging the new transformer based approach and fine-tune it to obtain quality results for the two above-mentioned tasks. Our results showed that a token classification approach towards the task of segmentation helps the model perform better and results in state-of-the-art scores.

We are also currently working on developing a curated dataset and model for the connective identification task for the Hindi language. This aims to increase the diversity of the available data and add a dataset to the existing corpora.

References

Stergos Afantenos, Pascal Denis, Philippe Muller, and Laurence Danlos. 2010. Learning recursive segments for discourse parsing. *arXiv preprint arXiv:1003.5372.*

Maria Jesus Aranzabe, Aitziber Atutxa, Kepa Bengoetxea, Arantza Diaz de Ilarraza, Iakes Goenaga, Koldo Gojenola, and Larraitz Uria. 2015. Automatic conversion of the basque dependency treebank to universal dependencies. In *Proceedings of the fourteenth international workshop on treebanks an linguistic theories (TLT14)*, pages 233–241.

Nicholas Asher, Julie Hunter, Mathieu Morey, Farah Benamara, and Stergos Afantenos. 2016. Discourse structure and dialogue acts in multiparty dialogue: the stac corpus. In *10th International Conference on Language Resources and Evaluation (LREC 2016)*, pages 2721–2727.

Nicholas Asher and Alex Lascarides. 2003. *Segmented Discourse Representation Theory: Dynamic Semantics With Discourse Structure.* Cambridge University Press.

Chloé Braud, Ophélie Lacroix, and Anders Søgaard. 2017a. Cross-lingual and cross-domain discourse segmentation of entire documents. *arXiv preprint arXiv:1704.04100.*

Chloé Braud, Ophélie Lacroix, and Anders Søgaard. 2017b. Does syntax help discourse segmentation? not so much. In *Conference on Empirical Methods in Natural Language Processing*, pages 2432–2442.

Shuyuan Cao, Iria da Cunha, and Mikel Iruskieta. 2018. The rst spanish-chinese treebank. In *Proceedings of the Joint Workshop on Linguistic Annotation, Multiword Expressions and Constructions (LAW-MWE-CxG-2018)*, pages 156–166.

Paula CF Cardoso, Erick G Maziero, Mara Luca Castro Jorge, Eloize MR Seno, Ariani Di Felippo, Lucia Helena Machado Rino, Maria das Gracas Volpe Nunes, and Thiago AS Pardo. 2011. Cstnews-a discourse-annotated corpus for single and multi-document summarization of news texts in brazilian portuguese. In *Proceedings of the 3rd RST Brazilian Meeting*, pages 88–105.

Lynn Carlson, Daniel Marcu, and Mary Ellen Okurowski. 2003. Building a discourse-tagged corpus in the framework of rhetorical structure theory. In *Current and new directions in discourse and dialogue*, pages 85–112. Springer.

Iria Da Cunha, Eric San Juan, Juan Manuel Torres-Moreno, Marina Lloberese, and Irene Castellóne. 2012. Diseg 1.0: The first system for spanish discourse segmentation. *Expert Systems with Applications*, 39(2):1671–1678.

Iria Da Cunha, Juan-Manuel Torres-Moreno, and Gerardo Sierra. 2011. On the development of the rst spanish treebank. In *Proceedings of the 5th Linguistic Annotation Workshop*, pages 1–10.

Jacob Devlin, Ming-Wei Chang, Kenton Lee, and Kristina Toutanova. 2018. BERT: pre-training of deep bidirectional transformers for language understanding. *CoRR*, abs/1810.04805.

Vanessa Wei Feng and Graeme Hirst. 2014. A linear-time bottom-up discourse parser with constraints and post-editing. In *Proceedings of the 52nd Annual Meeting of the Association for Computational Linguistics (Volume 1: Long Papers)*, pages 511–521.

Seeger Fisher and Brian Roark. 2007. The utility of parse-derived features for automatic discourse segmentation. In *Proceedings of the 45th Annual Meeting of the Association of Computational Linguistics*, pages 488–495.

Sepp Hochreiter and Jürgen Schmidhuber. 1997. Long short-term memory. *Neural computation*, 9(8):1735–1780.

M Iruskieta, MJ Aranzabe, A Diaz de Ilarraza, I Gonzalez, M Lersundi, and O Lopez de la Calle. 2013. Euskal rsttreebanka (euskal rst-ko erlazio eta zuhaitz bankua). the rst basque treebank: an online search interface to check rhetorical relations. In *4th Workshop "RST and Discourse Studies", Brasil.*

Mikel Iruskieta and Benat Zapirain. 2015. Euseduseg: A dependency-based edu segmentation for basque. *Procesamiento del Lenguaje Natural*, (55):41–48.

Rohit Jain and Dipti Misra Sharma. 2016. Explicit argument identification for discourse parsing in hindi: A hybrid pipeline. In *Proceedings of the NAACL Student Research Workshop*, pages 66–72.

Yangfeng Ji and Jacob Eisenstein. 2014. Representation learning for text-level discourse parsing. In *Proceedings of the 52nd annual meeting of the association for computational linguistics (volume 1: Long papers)*, pages 13–24.

Dan Jurafsky and James H. Martin. 2009. *Speech and language processing : an introduction to natural language processing, computational linguistics, and speech recognition.* Pearson Prentice Hall, Upper Saddle River, N.J.

Omri Koshorek, Adir Cohen, Noam Mor, Michael Rotman, and Jonathan Berant. 2018. Text segmentation as a supervised learning task. *arXiv preprint arXiv:1803.09337.*

Huong Le Thanh, Geetha Abeysinghe, and Christian Huyck. 2004. Generating discourse structures for written text. In *COLING 2004: Proceedings of the 20th International Conference on Computational Linguistics*, pages 329–335.

Jing Li, Aixin Sun, and Shafiq R Joty. 2018. Segbot: A generic neural text segmentation model with pointer network. In *IJCAI*, pages 4166–4172.

Qi Li, Tianshi Li, and Baobao Chang. 2016. Discourse parsing with attention-based hierarchical neural networks. In *Proceedings of EMNLP 2016*, pages 362–371.

Michal Lukasik, Boris Dadachev, Gonçalo Simoes, and Kishore Papineni. 2020. Text segmentation by cross segment attention. *arXiv preprint arXiv:2004.14535.*

Harald Lüngen, Csilla Puskás, Maja Bärenfänger, Mirco Hilbert, and Henning Lobin. 2006. Discourse segmentation of german written texts. In *International Conference on Natural Language Processing (in Finland)*, pages 245–256. Springer.

William C. Mann and Sandra A. Thompson. 1988. Rhetorical structure theory: Toward a functional theory of text organization. *Text*, 8:243–281.

Philippe Muller, Chloé Braud, and Mathieu Morey. 2019. Tony: Contextual embeddings for accurate multilingual discourse segmentation of full documents. In *Proceedings of the Workshop on Discourse Relation Parsing and Treebanking 2019*, pages 115–124. Association for Computational Linguistics.

Umangi Oza, Rashmi Prasad, Sudheer Kolachina, Dipti Misra Sharma, and Aravind Joshi. 2009. The hindi discourse relation bank. In *Proceedings of the Third Linguistic Annotation Workshop (LAW III)*, pages 158–161.

Thiago Alexandre Salgueiro Pardo and Maria das Graças Volpe Nunes. 2008. On the development and evaluation of a brazilian portuguese discourse parser. *Journal of Technical and Applied Informatics*, 15(2):43–64.

Marie-Paule Péry-Woodley, Stergos Afantenos, Lydia-Mai Ho-Dac, and Nicholas Asher. 2011. La ressource annodis, un corpus enrichi d'annotations discursives. *Traitement Automatique des Langues*, 52(3):71–101.

Emily Pitler and Ani Nenkova. 2009. Using syntax to disambiguate explicit discourse connectives in text.

Rashmi Prasad, Nikhil Dinesh, Alan Lee, Eleni Miltsakaki, Livio Robaldo, Aravind Joshi, and Bonnie Webber. 2008. The Penn Discourse Treebank 2.0. In *Proceedings of LREC*.

Gisela Redeker, Ildikó Berzlánovich, Nynke Van Der Vliet, Gosse Bouma, and Markus Egg. 2012. Multi-layer discourse annotation of a dutch text corpus. *age*, 1:2.

Sara Shahmohammadi, Hadi Veisi, and Ali Darzi. 2021. Persian rhetorical structure theory. *arXiv preprint arXiv:2106.13833*.

Radu Soricut and Daniel Marcu. 2003. Sentence level discourse parsing using syntactic and lexical information. In *Proceedings of the 2003 Human Language Technology Conference of the North American Chapter of the Association for Computational Linguistics*, pages 228–235.

Caroline Sporleder and Mirella Lapata. 2005. Discourse chunking and its application to sentence compression. In *Proceedings of Human Language Technology Conference and Conference on Empirical Methods in Natural Language Processing*, pages 257–264.

Manfred Stede and Arne Neumann. 2014. Potsdam commentary corpus 2.0: Annotation for discourse research. In *LREC*, pages 925–929.

Rajen Subba and Barbara Di Eugenio. 2007. Automatic discourse segmentation using neural networks. In *Proc. of the 11th Workshop on the Semantics and Pragmatics of Dialogue*, pages 189–190.

Milan Tofiloski, Julian Brooke, and Maite Taboada. 2009. A syntactic and lexical-based discourse segmenter. In *Proceedings of the ACL-IJCNLP 2009 conference short papers*, pages 77–80.

Svetlana Toldova, Dina Pisarevskaya, Margarita Ananyeva, Maria Kobozeva, Alexander Nasedkin, Sofia Nikiforova, Irina Pavlova, and Alexey Shelepov. 2017. Rhetorical relations markers in russian rst treebank. In *Proceedings of the 6th Workshop on Recent Advances in RST and Related Formalisms*, pages 29–33.

Nynke van der Vliet. 2010. Syntax-based discourse segmentation of dutch text. *Proceedings of the 15th Student Session, ESSLLI*, pages 203–210.

Ashish Vaswani, Noam Shazeer, Niki Parmar, Jakob Uszkoreit, Llion Jones, Aidan N Gomez, Łukasz Kaiser, and Illia Polosukhin. 2017. Attention is all you need. In *Advances in neural information processing systems*, pages 5998–6008.

Yizhong Wang, Sujian Li, and Jingfeng Yang. 2018. Toward fast and accurate neural discourse segmentation. *arXiv preprint arXiv:1808.09147*.

Jingfeng Yang and Sujian Li. 2018. Chinese discourse segmentation using bilingual discourse commonality. *arXiv preprint arXiv:1809.01497*.

Amir Zeldes. 2017. The gum corpus: Creating multilayer resources in the classroom. *Language Resources and Evaluation*, 51(3):581–612.

Amir Zeldes, Debopam Das, Erick Galani Maziero, Juliano Desiderato Antonio, and Mikel Iruskieta. 2019. The DISRPT 2019 Shared Task on Elementary Discourse Unit Segmentation and Connective Detection. In *Proceedings of the Workshop on Discourse Relation Parsing and Treebanking*.

Deniz Zeyrek and Murathan Kurfalı. 2017. Tdb 1.1: Extensions on turkish discourse bank. In *Proceedings of the 11th Linguistic Annotation Workshop*, pages 76–81.

Yuping Zhou and Nianwen Xue. 2015. The chinese discourse treebank: a chinese corpus annotated with discourse relations. *Language Resources and Evaluation*, 49(2):397–431.

Multi-lingual Discourse Segmentation and Connective Identification: MELODI at DISRPT2021

Morteza Ezzabady and **Philippe Muller** and **Chloé Braud**
IRIT, University of Toulouse, CNRS, ANITI

Abstract

We present an approach for discourse segmentation and discourse connective identification, both at the sentence and document level, within the DISRPT 2021 shared task, a multi-lingual and multi-formalism evaluation campaign.[1] Building on the most successful architecture from the 2019 similar shared task, we leverage datasets in the same or similar languages to augment training data and improve on the best systems from the previous campaign on 3 out of 4 subtasks, with a mean improvement on all 16 datasets of 0.85%. Within the Disrpt 21 campaign the system ranks 3rd overall, very close to the 2nd system, but with a significant gap with respect to the best system, which uses a rich set of additional features. The system is nonetheless the best on languages that benefited from cross-lingual training on sentence internal segmentation (German and Spanish).

1 Introduction

Discourse segmentation, the separation of a text or conversation in elementary units that make up the arguments of the rhetorical structure of a text, has long been a neglected step in discourse analysis, considered easy and generally assumed as given in discourse parsing studies, where the focus is to predict the rhetorical structure of a document, a labelled relational structure, with properties dependent on the theorerical framework considered, Rhetorical Structure Theory (RST, Mann and Thompson, 1988), Segmented Discourse Representation Theory (SDRT, Asher and Lascarides, 2003), or the Penn Discourse Treebank (PDTB, Prasad et al., 2008).

However this important step has generated more interest recently, as illustrated by the 2019 shared task at the Discourse Relation Parsing and Treebanking (DISRPT) workshop (Zeldes et al., 2019). This campaign made available several existing corpora in different language in a common format, expressing the task as a sequence tagging problem, where tokens are to be classified as beginning a segment or not, or, in the case of PDTB corpora, being part of a discourse connective signalling a relation between textual arguments. Segmentation in itself has also shown a lot of potential as an auxiliary task in machine translation (Chen et al., 2020) and summarization (Xu et al., 2020), independently of discourse parsing.

DISRPT 2021 shared task reproduces the same setting as DISRPT 2019, with some additional data and minor modifications of the original datasets, segmentation as task 1, connective identification as task 2, and adds the prediction of relations between segments, assuming those are known, as task 3.

The following shows examples from the English datasets, illustrating respectively task 1 and task 2, with intended units to recover marked between brackets:

- *[Three seats currently are vacant] [and three others are likely to be filled within a few years] (...)*
- *[But] [in the end] his resignation as Chancellor of the Exchequer may be a good thing (...)*

In the first case, tokens "Three" and "and" would be marked as segment beginnings. In the second case, where the target connectives are "but" and "in the end", beginning tokens "but" and "in" would be marked "B" (begin) and "the", "end", would be marked as "I" (inside). In both examples, other tokens would be marked "out".

Since sentences are almost always discourse units in existing frameworks, segmentation can be seen as two sub-problems: detecting sentences, and detecting intra-sentence segment boundaries. To reflect this, the 2019 shared task introduced two

[1] Note that authors Philippe Muller and Chloé Braud were part of the organization of the shared task.

Proceedings of the 2nd Shared Task on Discourse Relation Parsing and Treebanking (DISRPT 2021), pages 22–32
November 11, 2021. ©2021 Association for Computational Linguistics

sub-tasks for segmentation and connective identification: either sentence-level segmentation, with sentence boundaries given (when annotated, or provided with a sentence splitter otherwise), also informed by syntactic parsing of sentences, or without any of that information.

With the exception of systems presented at DISRPT 2019 (Bourgonje and Schäfer, 2019; Yu et al., 2019; Muller et al., 2019), existing work on segmentation always assumed gold sentences, e.g. (Wang et al., 2018; Lukasik et al., 2020).

One interesting aspect of such a task is the availability of comparable data in different languages. This has been leveraged in the past for segmentation (Braud et al., 2017b), but not in the past 2019 campaign, where the best system relied on fine-tuning a contextual language model for each language separately, albeit using the same multilingual embedding model (Muller et al., 2019).

Here we propose to build on the previous DISRPT best system and exploit the availability of multiple corpora for the same language, or the same family of languages (romance, germanic) to augment training of dedicated models.

Combining this approach with a few adjustments to the base model, we manage to improve on many datasets compare to the previous best DISRPT systems, with a mean difference in F1 score of 0.46% and 1.24% on segment boundary detection for sentence and document level respectively, and 3.07% on connective detection for sentences (we didn't improve results at document level for discourse connectives).

Within the Disrpt 21 campaign the system ranks 3rd overall, very close to the 2nd system, but with a significant gap with respect to the best system, which uses a rich set of additional features.

Our code and instructions to reproduce the experiments are available online.[2]

2 Related work

Discourse segmentation appeared as an NLP task with the creation of the first annotated RST documents in English, and was primarily rule-based (Marcu, 2000). Since then the literature on discourse parsing generally assumed that elementary discourse units (discourse segments) were given, with only a handful of exceptions (Soricut and Marcu, 2003; Fisher and Roark, 2007; Tofiloski et al., 2009; Hernault et al., 2010; Joty et al., 2015), until more recent neural-based work (Wang et al., 2018; Lukasik et al., 2020), still at the sentence level, and always on English or Mandarin. Only the work of (Braud et al., 2017b,c) have considered more varied languages, after the creation of a few different datasets in the past ten years (see the Data section below).

The DISRPT 2019 workshop introduced a more general evaluation framework for discourse segmentation with a shared task considering multilingual data, and segmentation both at the sentence and document level (Zeldes et al., 2019). The best system (Muller et al., 2019) at both granularities (sentence and document) used a sequential tagging model fine-tuned on contextual embeddings.

Multi-lingual discourse parsing is also becoming more popular, see for instance (Braud et al., 2017a; Chen et al., 2020), in which it is seen as a form of multi-task learning problem, but this was not applied to discourse segmentation. In other NLP subfields, leveraging availability of corpora in different languages for the same tasks is an active area of research, with different strategies for combining tasks and languages, using meta-learning and complex sampling strategies (Nooralahzadeh et al., 2020; Tarunesh et al., 2021). A simpler approach that inspired us here, due to (Dehouck and Denis, 2019), is to use the relations between close languages to guide the training process on a task: a generic model is trained on groups of languages, further refined with models by subgroups and finally fine-tuned on individual languages.

3 Data

The 2021 shared task provides 16 corpora annotated either with discourse boundaries (13) or discourse connectives in the case of PDTB corpora (3), with the RST Farsi corpus as a surprise dataset. This covers 11 different languages, mostly indo-european languages, and with a majority of european languages: 3 romance (Spanish, French, Portuguese), 3 germanic (English, German, Dutch), Russian, the only non indo-european being Turkish, Basque, and Mandarin. Some of the datasets depend on licences for the underlying text corpus, and are not freely available. We had licences for all of them except the Mandarin corpus (zho.pdtb.cdtb), provided by the organizers for the evaluation of the task. Except Farsi, all the datasets were present in the DISRPT 2019 shared task, but the russian

[2] https://gitlab.irit.fr/melodi/andiamo/discoursesegmentation/discut

Corpus	Lang	# Doc. Train	Dev	Test	Sent seg	# Sents. Train	# Units Train
Connectives — PDTB							
eng.pdtb.pdtb	en	1,992	79	91	manual	44,563	23,850
tur.pdtb.tdb	tr	159	19	19	manual	25,080	6,841
zho.pdtb.cdtb	zh	125	21	18	manual	2,049	1,034
EDUs — RST							
eng.rst.rstdt	en	309	38	38	manual	6,672	17,646
eng.rst.gum	en	78	18	18	manual	3,600	5,012
deu.rst.pcc	de	142	17	17	manual	1,773	2,449
eus.rst.ert	eu	84	28	28	manual	991	1,713
far.rst.prstc	far	120	15	15	stanza	1713	4607
nld.rst.nldt	nl	56	12	12	manual	1,202	1,679
por.rst.cstn	pt	110	14	12	manual	1,595	3,916
rus.rst.rrt	ru	272	30	30	stanza	18932	34682
spa.rst.stb	es	203	32	32	manual	1,577	2,474
spa.rst.sctb	es	32	9	9	manual	304	473
zho.rst.sctb	zh	32	9	9	manual	344	473
EDUs — SDRT							
eng.sdrt.stac	en	29	6	6	manual	7,689	8,843
fra.sdrt.annodis	fr	64	11	11	manual	880	2,411

Table 1: Descriptions of all corpora, according to the underlying theoretical framework. The tasks consist in finding connectives in the PDTB datasets, or the Elementary Discourse Units (segments) in RST and SDRT datasets. For each corpora are listed the number of documents in each split, the number of sentences and annotated units (connective tokens or segment boundaries in the training set, and whether the gold sentences were manually annotated or given by a parser.

dataset has been extended since, and some corpora without gold syntax annotations have been reparsed with Stanza or Spacy to provide morpho-syntaxic information for the sentence-internal subtasks.

All tasks are considered as sequence tagging, and annotated as such: for segmentation, each token is marked as being a segment boudary or not, and for connectives, which can span multiple tokens, the annotation follows the BIO convention with three labels Begin/Inside/Out for each token.

Datasets are not homogenous, as they were annotated along different principles based on three competing theoretical frameworks:

- Rhetorical Structure Theory (Mann and Thompson, 1988), which assumes a linear segmentation of documents in discourse units (no overlaps), which are then related in constituant tree structures. This is followed in the majority of corpora (11).

- Segmented Discrouse Representation Theory (Asher and Lascarides, 2003), which allows for embedded segments, and were linearized here for homogeneity of the task: a segment embedded in another one was re-annotated as forming 3 three segments. This is the case of two corpora.

- Penn Discourse Treebank (Prasad et al., 2008), which annotates discourse connectives and their arguments in a discourse relation. This gives rise to a different annotation scheme as noted above, as the task is only to locate the connective.

Table 1 presents the size of all corpora, separated by theoretical framework, and expressed in number of documents, number of sentences, and number of discourse units (segments or connectives). Note that the different corpora greatly vary in sizes and annotations. One dataset is annotated on chat conversations (STAC), while all the others are on written text, mostly news or encyclopedic.

Experimental results cannot be compared to previous multi-lingual segmentation efforts (Braud et al., 2017b), because some of the corpora have been revised (Gum, RRT) or not taken entirely (CSTN), and some have been added (TDB, PRSTC), but should be quite close to the DISRPT 2019 evaluation, as only the Russian and the GUM corpora have been extended (and there is an additional dataset).

More details can be found about all datasets

in the following publications: English RSTDT (Carlson et al., 2001), PDTB (Prasad et al., 2008), SDRT-STAC (Asher et al., 2016) and GUM (Zeldes, 2016), Spanish RST (2)(da Cunha et al., 2011; Cao et al., 2018) Mandarin Chinese (Zhou et al., 2014; Cao et al., 2018), German RST (Stede and Neumann, 2014), French SDRT-Annodis (Afantenos et al., 2012), Basque RST (Iruskieta et al., 2013), Portuguese RST (Cardoso et al., 2011), Russian RST (Pisarevskaya et al., 2017), Turkish PDTB (Zeyrek et al., 2013) Dutch RST (Redeker et al., 2012) and Persian RST (Shahmohammadi et al., 2021).

4 Approach

In this paper we want to leverage combinations of multiple datasets for training, not only with corpora for the same language and task, but also with languages from the same families.

4.1 Base architecture

We started from the architecture that showed the best results on almost all languages and configurations at DISRPT 2019, namely (Muller et al., 2019), which is built around BERT (Devlin et al., 2019), a contextual language model that is easy to fine-tune on sequence tagging problems. The original architecture combined BERT contextual embeddings to the output of CNN filters over characters of each word piece, that were then fed to single-layer BiLSTM layer for the final prediction. The model is initialized with the multilingual BERT model, then fine-tune on all corpora separately as sequence tagging tasks. The original implementation used the AllenNLP library (Gardner et al., 2017), and so does our implementation.

Since BERT has a limitation on the number of word pieces it can take as input, a preprocessing step must be taken for document-level segmentation. In (Muller et al., 2019), the core-nlp library was used to predict sentence boundaries, and use this information, while we used the more recent Stanza library by the same team for that purpose (Qi et al., 2020).

We explored potential improvements for that architecture, swapping the multi-lingual pretrained language model XLM (Conneau and Lample, 2019), or adding another layer to the BiLSTM stage. The final configuration was chosen based on preliminary experiments on some of the datasets, evaluated on their respective development sets. They showed that XLM didn't help, but the extra layer of LSTM could. Changes to other hyperparameters didn't improve these preliminary results so we kept them as in the original model. Details of the parameters can be found in the declarative config file of the model, also added as supplementary material.

Input	Corpus	P	R	F1
conll	deu.rst.pcc	92.58	95.27	93.91
	eng.rst.gum	94.06	90.19	92.08
	eng.rst.rstdt	96.35	95.38	95.86
	eng.sdrt.stac	94.19	95.49	94.84
	eus.rst.ert	87.23	83.75	85.46
	fas.rst.prstc	91.18	91.49	91.33
	fra.sdrt.annodis	87.13	90.11	88.59
	nld.rst.nldt	95.52	93.29	94.40
	por.rst.cstn	90.63	92.06	91.34
	rus.rst.rrt	86.04	83.83	84.92
	spa.rst.rststb	91.80	93.56	92.67
	spa.rst.sctb	85.57	80.58	83.00
	zho.rst.sctb	93.02	77.67	84.66
	mean	91.18	89.44	90.24
doc	deu.rst.pcc	94.51	93.82	94.16
	eng.rst.gum	91.80	91.68	91.74
	eng.rst.rstdt	93.48	94.94	94.20
	eng.sdrt.stac	86.10	87.52	86.81
	eus.rst.ert	87.56	85.23	86.38
	fas.rst.prstc	91.21	91.84	91.52
	fra.sdrt.annodis	87.52	90.83	89.14
	nld.rst.nldt	93.91	94.46	94.19
	por.rst.cstn	92.43	91.11	91.77
	rus.rst.rrt	83.09	81.65	82.37
	spa.rst.rststb	92.54	94.75	93.63
	spa.rst.sctb	73.23	90.29	80.87
	zho.rst.sctb	64.18	83.50	72.57
	mean	87.04	90.12	88.41

Table 2: Segmentation results on the development sets, for both sentence (conll) and document (doc) levels.

4.2 Dataset grouping

Since the shared task involves multiple datasets with the same language (2 for Spanish RST, 2 for English RST), we assumed it would be beneficial to combine them for training. Datasets in the same language are not necessarily consistent in their annotation, but we hypothetize that they have enough commonalities to help training. We also took inspiration from work on multi-lingual syntactic parsing where a lot of corpora follow the same formalism, and where past work has tried to use commonalities between different languages, particularly the approach of (Dehouck and Denis, 2019) in which the phylogenic tree of languages guides the training process: a generic model is trained on groups of languages, further refined in models by subgroups and finally fine-tuned on individual languages. DISRPT datasets are not numerous enough to provide a complex tree of languages, but we can still take advantage of the presence of languages that are relatively close: romance languages (3 languages and 4 datasets for segmentation), germanic languages (3 languages and 5 datasets for segmentation).

Input	Corpus	P	R	F1
conll	eng.pdtb.pdtb	92.27	88.55	90.37
	tur.pdtb.tdb	80.54	84.50	82.47
	zho.pdtb.cdtb	77.54	72.94	75.17
	mean	83.45	82.00	82.67
doc	eng.pdtb.pdtb	93.00	89.86	91.40
	tur.pdtb.tdb	80.66	85.66	83.08
	zho.pdtb.cdtb	71.27	64.69	67.82
	mean	81.64	80.07	80.77

Table 3: Connective identification results on the development sets, for both sentence (conll) and document (doc).

5 Results

5.1 Base model

The modification of ToNy, the best system from DISRPT 2019, gives us our base system on which we will build with multi-corpora training in a second stage.

We report the results of these systems on segmentation in Table 2, and on discourse connectives identification in Table 3, with precision, recall and F1 score on the detection of segment boundary tokens, and discourse connectives. A first comparison with respect to each best subsystem from 2019 for the 4 subtasks is given in Table 6. That means ToNy for segmentation (both intra-sentential and plain), discourse connectives (plain), and Gumdrop for discourse connectives (Conll input). We can see that on average on all datasets, the base system gains +0.5, mostly due to its improvements on the plain document segmentation (connective detection only involves 3 datasets). We left out the surprise dataset for 2021 from that evaluation, since we do not have a comparison point. Note that results on this new dataset are good and consistent with the other corpora. Lower results are obtained on smaller datasets for obvious reasons (Spanish sctb, Chinese Mandarin sctb, and to a lesser extent Basque and French). Models trained without sentence information perform a little worse, as expected, with -1.6% on average, again with wider gaps for small corpora.

We do not show the breakup by dataset for the comparison with DISRPT 2019, but there is a lot of variances in results, with differences ranging from -4.5 (French Annodis) to +6.85 (Mandarin SCTB), and not necessarily only on small corpora.

Corpus	Group	P	R	F1
spa/rststb	self	91.80	93.56	92.67
	SPA	94.24	93.79	94.02
	SPO	93.81	94.03	93.92
	ROM	93.66	91.65	92.64
	FT	94.30	94.75	**94.52**
spa/sctb	self	85.57	80.58	83.00
	SPA	83.64	89.32	86.38
	SPO	86.24	91.26	**88.68**
	ROM	81.98	88.35	85.05
	FT	88.89	85.44	87.13
por/cstn	self	90.63	92.06	91.34
	SPO	92.88	89.05	90.92
	ROM	90.14	90.00	90.07
	FT	90.98	92.86	**91.91**
fra/annodis	self	87.13	90.11	**88.59**
	ROM	91.12	83.09	86.92

Table 4: Intra sentential results on romance development datasets, with different training setups: SPA means the grouping of both spanish datasets for training, SPO the grouping of spanish and portuguese data, ROM the addition of French to the group. FT means a model fine-tuning the SPO model. Lines with "self" are just copied from the basic evaluation (training on the dataset only) for comparison. In bold are indicated the best F1 results per dataset on their development set, and the corresponding model was thus kept for the final evaluation.

5.2 Multi-dataset training

As shown above, a lot of smaller datasets have lower results than larger ones, which is to be expected. We present here the result when applying the strategy described in Section 4.2. We tried it on two groups of languages: romance languages, and germanic languages.

For romance languages, since there are two spanish RST corpora, we grouped them to trained a "spanish" more generic model, then we trained a model with all Spanish and Portuguese data, then a generic romance model by including also French. We then used those models for predictions on the datasets respective development part. We did something similar with germanic languages, grouping all English datasets into one, joining the Dutch and German datasets into another one, and finally training a generic germanic model on all of them. Following a procedure similar to what was done in (Dehouck and Denis, 2019), we also fine-tuned some of these models on the individual datasets before using them for prediction. Lack of time during the campaign prevented us from trying all combinations and all datasets like this, but we tested this on all Spanish and English datasets, respectively fine-tuning the global Spanish-Portuguese on Spanish and Portuguese datasets (since it showed a good compromise on the dev sets) and the global English model on all English datasets. Due to time constraints, we tested this only on one type of input, the sentence level (conll files).

Results are presented in Tables 4 and 5. For the final evaluation, we kept for each dataset the model that performed better on the dataset development test.

Corpus	Group	P	R	F1
deu.rst.pcc	self	92.58	95.27	93.91
	GD	95.51	92.73	94.10
	GER	96.64	94.18	**95.40**
nld.rst.nldt	self	95.52	93.29	94.40
	GD	96.95	92.71	**94.78**
	GER	94.44	94.17	94.31
eng.rst.gum	self	94.06	90.19	92.08
	ENG	94.08	92.64	**93.36**
	GER	94.11	92.42	93.26
	FT	93.63	92.12	92.87
eng.rst.rstdt	self	96.35	95.38	**95.86**
	ENG	96.27	94.77	95.51
	GER	95.47	95.10	95.29
	FT	94.96	96.55	95.75
eng.sdrt.stac	self	94.19	95.49	94.84
	ENG	95.80	92.81	94.28
	GER	95.98	93.07	94.50
	FT	95.55	94.97	**95.26**

Table 5: Intra sentential results on germanic development datasets, with different training setups: GD means the grouping of German and Dutch for training, GER the grouping of English, German and Dutch, and ENG the grouping of all 3 English datasets. FT means a model fine-tuning the global ENG model on the specific corpus training set. Lines with "self" are just copied from the basic evaluation (training on the dataset only) for comparison. In bold are indicated the best F1 results per dataset on their development set.

5.3 Final evaluation

For the final evaluation of the campaign, every team provided their code and instructions for reproducing the experiments, and one member of the organization team reproduced entirely the experiments of one model they were not involved with (two of the four teams involved organization members, including the present system).

We reported the official scores on the test sets in Tables 7 for segmentation and 8 for connective detection.

Overall our system is ranked 3rd out of 4, with results very close to the 2nd-ranked system (Segformers), with only 0.15% difference on average for treebanked data segmentation, and 0.45% on plain data segmentation. The gap with the first ranked system (DiscoDisco) is 0.7% on average on treebanked segmentation and 1.28% on plain text segmentation. Our system performed less well on connective detection, especially with respect to models taking dependency between labels into account (such as a CRF in the case of DiscoDisco): about 4.5% less than Segformers and 6% less than DiscoDisco, mostly due to lower results on the Mandarin dataset.[3]

It is to be noted that we achieved our best results in relation to the other systems with datasets used in cross-training with similar languages (see Sections 4.2 and 5.2), and for which we observed on the development data that it had an impact: German and Spanish corpora, in the case of treebanked data (conll), since we didn't have time to try this strategy

[3]Full results for all systems are not shown for space constraint reasons, but are displayed on the Shared task website at `https://sites.google.com/georgetown.edu/disrpt2021/results` and are summarized in the introductory paper to the Shared Task proceedings.

task	input	Δbase/19	Δ grouped/19
pdtb	conll	3.07	3.07
pdtb	tok	-1.31	-1.31
seg	connl	-0.41	0.46
seg	tok	1.24	1.24
all	all	0.51	0.85

Table 6: Mean comparison of our base system and our improved system with respect to the best Disrpt 2019 system for each sub task, and the mean on all 16 datasets. This is the only evaluation we made on the test set prior to the official evaluation. Note that grouped training was tested only on conll segmentation, so the other scores are just copied from the base system.

on plain documents. We have the best scores on these languages, but note that cross-training cannot really explain the good results on German, since results are surprisingly similar between treebanked and plain data.

6 Conclusion

We presented an approach for discourse segmentation and discourse connective identification, both at the sentence and document level, in a multi-lingual and multi-formalism context. Building on the successful architecture from the 2019 DISRPT shared task, we leverage datasets in the same or similar languages to augment training data and improve on the best systems from the previous campaign, on 3 of the 4 sub-tasks. While below the best system which uses a rich set of features over a similar architecture, we still manage to have the best scores on some of the languages where we experimented with cross-lingual training: German and Spanish for sentence-internal segmentation.

Due to time constraints, we could not fully explore all potentially useful language combinations and fine-tuning on specific datasets, that could help improve on the tasks, and give insights on how different languages help each other addressing the discourse segmentation problem. Further progress on multi-lingual embeddings or alignments of different embeddings could be a source of future investigations, as well as more elaborate multi-lingual training procedures.

Acknowledgments

This work was partially supported by the ANR (ANR-19-PI3A-0004) through the AI Interdisciplinary Institute, ANITI, as a part of France's "Investing for the Future — PIA3" program, and through the project SLANT (ANR-19-CE23-0022) and Quantum (ANR-19-CE23-0025).

treebanked	P	R	F1
deu.rst.pcc	98.91	92.52	**95.61**
eng.rst.gum	93.27	93.65	93.46
eng.rst.rstdt	96.16	95.99	96.08
eng.sdrt.stac	97.41	92.37	94.82
eus.rst.ert	90.04	83.11	86.44
fas.rst.prstc	93.54	90.75	92.12
fra.sdrt.annodis	87.26	88.67	87.96
nld.rst.nldt	94.15	95.27	94.71
por.rst.cstn	90.31	94.44	92.33
rus.rst.rrt	88.19	81.10	84.50
spa.rst.rststb	92.04	93.04	**92.54**
spa.rst.sctb	85.39	90.48	**87.86**
zho.rst.sctb	92.48	73.21	81.73
mean	92.24	89.58	90.78
plain	P	R	F1
deu.rst.pcc	94.67	96.60	**95.63**
eng.rst.gum	92.76	89.54	91.13
eng.rst.rstdt	93.39	94.50	93.94
eng.sdrt.stac	85.30	87.01	86.14
eus.rst.ert	91.45	83.78	87.45
fas.rst.prstc	93.59	89.40	91.45
fra.sdrt.annodis	89.90	86.41	88.12
nld.rst.nldt	94.35	93.79	94.07
por.rst.cstn	93.36	91.83	92.59
rus.rst.rrt	83.60	84.01	83.80
spa.rst.rststb	92.19	89.78	90.97
spa.rst.sctb	78.65	89.88	**83.89**
zho.rst.sctb	68.11	75.00	71.39
mean	88.56	88.58	88.51

Table 7: Final official segmentation results on the test set, reproduced by the organizers. In bold, F1 scores for which our system has the best performance of the shared task.

treebanked	P	R	F1
PDTB	93.32	88.67	90.94
TDB	90.55	86.93	88.70
CDTB	84.43	66.03	74.10
mean	89.43	80.54	84.58
plain			
PDTB	88.84	92.09	90.43
TDB	90.12	88.10	89.10
CDTB	77.40	72.44	74.83
mean	85.45	84.21	84.79

Table 8: Final official connective detection results on the test set, reproduced by the organizers.

References

Stergos Afantenos, Nicholas Asher, Farah Benamara, Myriam Bras, Cécile Fabre, Lydia-Mai Ho-Dac, Anne Le Draoulec, Philippe Muller, Marie-Paule Pery-Woodley, Laurent Prévot, Josette Rebeyrolles, Ludovic Tanguy, Marianne Vergez-Couret, and Laure Vieu. 2012. An empirical resource for discovering cognitive principles of discourse organisation: the annodis corpus. In *Proceedings of LREC*.

Nicholas Asher, Julie Hunter, Mathieu Morey, Farah Benamara, and Stergos Afantenos. 2016. Discourse structure and dialogue acts in multiparty dialogue: the stac corpus. In *Proceedings of LREC*.

Nicholas Asher and Alex Lascarides. 2003. *Logics of Conversation*. Cambridge University Press.

Peter Bourgonje and Robin Schäfer. 2019. Multilingual and cross-genre discourse unit segmentation. In *Proceedings of the Workshop on Discourse Relation Parsing and Treebanking 2019*, pages 105–114, Minneapolis, MN. Association for Computational Linguistics.

Chloé Braud, Maximin Coavoux, and Anders Søgaard. 2017a. Cross-lingual RST discourse parsing. In *Proceedings of the 15th Conference of the European Chapter of the Association for Computational Linguistics: Volume 1, Long Papers*, pages 292–304, Valencia, Spain. Association for Computational Linguistics.

Chloé Braud, Ophélie Lacroix, and Anders Søgaard. 2017b. Cross-lingual and cross-domain discourse segmentation of entire documents. In *Proceedings of the 55th Annual Meeting of the Association for Computational Linguistics (Volume 2: Short Papers)*, pages 237–243, Vancouver, Canada. Association for Computational Linguistics.

Chloé Braud, Ophélie Lacroix, and Anders Søgaard. 2017c. Does syntax help discourse segmentation? not so much. In *Proceedings of the 2017 Conference on Empirical Methods in Natural Language Processing*, pages 2432–2442, Copenhagen, Denmark. Association for Computational Linguistics.

Shuyuan Cao, Iria da Cunha, and Mikel Iruskieta. 2018. The RST spanish-chinese treebank. In *Proceedings of LAW-MWE-CxG*.

Paula C.F. Cardoso, Erick G. Maziero, María Lucía Castro Jorge, Eloize R.M. Seno, Ariani Di Felippo, Lucia Helena Machado Rino, Maria das Graças Volpe Nunes, and Thiago A. S. Pardo. 2011. CSTNews - a discourse-annotated corpus for single and multi-document summarization of news texts in Brazilian Portuguese. In *Proceedings of the 3rd RST Brazilian Meeting*, pages 88–105.

Lynn Carlson, Daniel Marcu, and Mary Ellen Okurowski. 2001. Building a discourse-tagged corpus in the framework of Rhetorical Structure Theory. In *Proceedings of the Second SIGdial Workshop on Discourse and Dialogue*.

Junxuan Chen, Xiang Li, Jiarui Zhang, Chulun Zhou, Jianwei Cui, Bin Wang, and Jinsong Su. 2020. Modeling discourse structure for document-level neural machine translation. In *Proceedings of the First Workshop on Automatic Simultaneous Translation*, pages 30–36, Seattle, Washington. Association for Computational Linguistics.

Alexis Conneau and Guillaume Lample. 2019. Cross-lingual language model pretraining. In *Advances in Neural Information Processing Systems 32: Annual Conference on Neural Information Processing Systems 2019, NeurIPS 2019, December 8-14, 2019, Vancouver, BC, Canada*, pages 7057–7067.

Iria da Cunha, Juan-Manuel Torres-Moreno, and Gerardo Sierra. 2011. On the development of the RST Spanish Treebank. In *Proceedings of the Fifth Linguistic Annotation Workshop, LAW*.

Mathieu Dehouck and Pascal Denis. 2019. Phylogenic multi-lingual dependency parsing. In *Proceedings of the 2019 Conference of the North American Chapter of the Association for Computational Linguistics: Human Language Technologies, Volume 1 (Long and Short Papers)*, pages 192–203, Minneapolis, Minnesota. Association for Computational Linguistics.

Jacob Devlin, Ming-Wei Chang, Kenton Lee, and Kristina Toutanova. 2019. BERT: Pre-training of deep bidirectional transformers for language understanding. In *Proceedings of the 2019 Conference of the North American Chapter of the Association for Computational Linguistics: Human Language Technologies, Volume 1 (Long and Short Papers)*, pages 4171–4186, Minneapolis, Minnesota. Association for Computational Linguistics.

Seeger Fisher and Brian Roark. 2007. The utility of parse-derived features for automatic discourse segmentation. In *Proceedings of the 45th Annual Meeting of the Association of Computational Linguistics*, pages 488–495, Prague, Czech Republic. Association for Computational Linguistics.

Matt Gardner, Joel Grus, Mark Neumann, Oyvind Tafjord, Pradeep Dasigi, Nelson F. Liu, Matthew Peters, Michael Schmitz, and Luke S. Zettlemoyer. 2017. Allennlp: A deep semantic natural language processing platform.

Hugo Hernault, Helmut Prendinger, David A. duVerle, and Mitsuru Ishizuka. 2010. HILDA: A discourse parser using support vector machine classification. *Dialogue Discourse*, 1(3):1–33.

Mikel Iruskieta, María J. Aranzabe, Arantza Diaz de Ilarraza, Itziar Gonzalez-Dios, Mikel Lersundi, and Oier Lopez de la Calle. 2013. The RST Basque Treebank: an online search interface to check rhetorical relations. In *Proceedings of the 4th Workshop RST and Discourse Studies*.

Shafiq Joty, Giuseppe Carenini, and Raymond T. Ng. 2015. CODRA: A novel discriminative framework for rhetorical analysis. *Computational Linguistics*, 41(3):385–435.

Michal Lukasik, Boris Dadachev, Kishore Papineni, and Gonçalo Simões. 2020. Text segmentation by cross segment attention. In *Proceedings of the 2020 Conference on Empirical Methods in Natural Language Processing (EMNLP)*, pages 4707–4716, Online. Association for Computational Linguistics.

William C. Mann and Sandra A. Thompson. 1988. Rhetorical Structure Theory: Toward a functional theory of text organization. *Text*, 8:243–281.

Daniel Marcu. 2000. The rhetorical parsing of unrestricted texts: a surface-based approach. *Computational Linguistics*, 26(3):395–448.

Philippe Muller, Chloé Braud, and Mathieu Morey. 2019. ToNy: Contextual embeddings for accurate multilingual discourse segmentation of full documents. In *Proceedings of the Workshop on Discourse Relation Parsing and Treebanking 2019*, pages 115–124, Minneapolis, MN. Association for Computational Linguistics.

Farhad Nooralahzadeh, Giannis Bekoulis, Johannes Bjerva, and Isabelle Augenstein. 2020. Zero-shot cross-lingual transfer with meta learning. In *Proceedings of the 2020 Conference on Empirical Methods in Natural Language Processing (EMNLP)*, pages 4547–4562, Online. Association for Computational Linguistics.

Dina Pisarevskaya, Margarita Ananyeva, Maria Kobozeva, A Nasedkin, S Nikiforova, I Pavlova, and A Shelepov. 2017. Towards building a discourse-annotated corpus of russian. In *Proceedings of the International Conference on Computational Linguistics and Intellectual Technologies "Dialogue"*.

Rashmi Prasad, Nikhil Dinesh, Alan Lee, Eleni Miltsakaki, Livio Robaldo, Aravind Joshi, and Bonnie Webber. 2008. The Penn Discourse Treebank 2.0. In *The Sixth International Conference on Language Resources and Evaluation*, pages 2961 – 2968, Marrakech, Morocco. ELRA.

Peng Qi, Yuhao Zhang, Yuhui Zhang, Jason Bolton, and Christopher D. Manning. 2020. Stanza: A Python natural language processing toolkit for many human languages. In *Proceedings of the 58th Annual Meeting of the Association for Computational Linguistics: System Demonstrations*.

Gisela Redeker, Ildikó Berzlánovich, Nynke van der Vliet, Gosse Bouma, and Markus Egg. 2012. Multilayer discourse annotation of a Dutch text corpus. In *Proceedings of LREC*.

Sara Shahmohammadi, Hadi Veisi, and Ali Darzi. 2021. Persian rhetorical structure theory. *CoRR*, abs/2106.13833.

Radu Soricut and Daniel Marcu. 2003. Sentence level discourse parsing using syntactic and lexical information. In *Proceedings of the 2003 Human Language Technology Conference of the North American Chapter of the Association for Computational Linguistics*, pages 228–235.

Manfred Stede and Arne Neumann. 2014. Potsdam Commentary Corpus 2.0: Annotation for discourse research. In *Proceedings of LREC*.

Ishan Tarunesh, Sushil Khyalia, Vishwajeet Kumar, Ganesh Ramakrishnan, and Preethi Jyothi. 2021. Meta-learning for effective multi-task and multilingual modelling. In *Proceedings of the 16th Conference of the European Chapter of the Association for Computational Linguistics: Main Volume*, pages 3600–3612, Online. Association for Computational Linguistics.

Milan Tofiloski, Julian Brooke, and Maite Taboada. 2009. A syntactic and lexical-based discourse segmenter. In *Proceedings of the ACL-IJCNLP 2009 Conference Short Papers*, pages 77–80, Suntec, Singapore. Association for Computational Linguistics.

Yizhong Wang, Sujian Li, and Jingfeng Yang. 2018. Toward fast and accurate neural discourse segmentation. In *Proceedings of the 2018 Conference on Empirical Methods in Natural Language Processing*, pages 962–967, Brussels, Belgium. Association for Computational Linguistics.

Jiacheng Xu, Zhe Gan, Yu Cheng, and Jingjing Liu. 2020. Discourse-aware neural extractive text summarization. In *Proceedings of the 58th Annual Meeting of the Association for Computational Linguistics*, pages 5021–5031, Online. Association for Computational Linguistics.

Yue Yu, Yilun Zhu, Yang Liu, Yan Liu, Siyao Peng, Mackenzie Gong, and Amir Zeldes. 2019. GumDrop at the DISRPT2019 shared task: A model stacking approach to discourse unit segmentation and connective detection. In *Proceedings of the Workshop on Discourse Relation Parsing and Treebanking 2019*, pages 133–143, Minneapolis, MN. Association for Computational Linguistics.

Amir Zeldes. 2016. The GUM corpus: Creating multilayer resources in the classroom. In *Proceedings of LREC*.

Amir Zeldes, Debopam Das, Erick Galani Maziero, Juliano Antonio, and Mikel Iruskieta. 2019. The DISRPT 2019 shared task on elementary discourse unit segmentation and connective detection. In *Proceedings of the Workshop on Discourse Relation Parsing and Treebanking 2019*, pages 97–104, Minneapolis, MN. Association for Computational Linguistics.

Deniz Zeyrek, Demirsahin Isın, A. Sevdik-Çallı, and Ruket Çakıcı. 2013. Turkish discourse bank: Porting a discourse annotation style to a morphologically rich language. *Dialogue and Discourse*.

Yuping Zhou, Jill Lu, Jennifer Zhang, and Nianwen Xue. 2014. Chinese discourse treebank 0.5 LDC2014T21. Web Download. Philadelphia: Linguistic Data Consortium.

Delexicalised Multilingual Discourse Segmentation for DISRPT 2021 and Tense, Mood, Voice and Modality Tagging for 11 Languages

Tillmann Dönicke
Göttingen Centre for Digital Humanities
University of Göttingen, Germany
tillmann.doenicke@uni-goettingen.de

Abstract

This paper describes our participating system for the Shared Task on Discourse Segmentation and Connective Identification across Formalisms and Languages. Key features of the presented approach are the formulation as a clause-level classification task, a language-independent feature inventory based on Universal Dependencies grammar, and composite-verb-form analysis. The achieved F1 is 92% for German and English and lower for other languages. The paper also presents a clause-level tagger for grammatical tense, aspect, mood, voice and modality in 11 languages.

1 Introduction

Despite the important role of discourse segmentation for natural language processing (NLP), there is no clear-cut definition of what a discourse segment is. Degand and Simon (2009) determine the boundaries of discourse segments as the intersection of clause boundaries and prosodic boundaries, which means specifically that a discourse segment spans one or several clauses (clauses as minimal discourse segments had been proposed in preceding works, e.g. Mann and Thompson (1988)). We follow this approach and view discourse segmentation as a binary classification problem that predicts for a clause whether it is the start of a new discourse segment. Working with only text makes it impossible to fully implement Degand and Simon (2009)'s approach and include features that capture prosody and prosodic change. Instead, we represent clauses as morphosyntactic feature structures that capture grammatical roles (subject, object etc.), verbal categories and clause connectives, believing that the use of pronouns, the change of tense, aspect and mood, the presence of conjunctions and other linguistic features also signal segment boundaries.

The shared task provides discourse-segmented treebanks for 11 languages. All datasets exist in the Universal Dependencies (UD) format (Nivre et al., 2016). UD grammar (UDG) builds on the idea that all natural languages can be described by a unique inventory of word categories and grammatical rules. Treebanks annotated in UDG thus share the same part-of-speech (POS) tags, morphological features (MFs) and dependency relations (DepRels), which encourages the development of multilingual applications. Things that still significantly differ between languages are the surface forms of words (obviously), the presence/absence of MFs and the order of words and constituents. To alleviate these dissimilarities, we will view sentences as delexicalised, unordered trees and assimilate morphosyntactic features between languages.

Dataset	Sents	Conn.	Delex.	WO
deu.rst.pcc	2,193	no	no	OV
eng.pdtb.pdtb	48,630	yes	yes	VO
eng.rst.gum	8,292	no	yes	–"–
eng.rst.rstdt	8,318	no	yes	–"–
eng.sdrt.stac	11,087	no	no	–"–
eus.rst.ert	2,380	no	no	OV
fas.rst.prstc	2,179	no	no	OV
fra.sdrt.annodis	1,507	no	no	VO
nld.rst.nldt	1,651	no	no	OV
por.rst.cstn	2,221	no	no	VO
rus.rst.rrt	23,044	no	no	VO
spa.rst.rststb	2,089	no	no	VO
spa.rst.sctb	516	no	no	–"–
tur.pdtb.cdtb	31,197	yes	yes	OV
zho.pdtb.cdtb	2,891	yes	yes	VO
zho.rst.sctb	580	no	no	–"–

Table 1: Datasets: total number of sentences, whether discourse connectives are annotated, whether surface forms have been removed, and basic word order.

2 Data and Task

Table 1 gives an overview of the available data. There are 16 datasets for 11 languages, but

Proceedings of the 2nd Shared Task on Discourse Relation Parsing and Treebanking (DISRPT 2021), pages 33–45
November 11, 2021. ©2021 Association for Computational Linguistics

the number of sentences for each dataset varies greatly, from 0.5k in `spa.rst.sctb` to 48.6k in `eng.pdtb.pdtb`.

In 13 of the datasets, only discourse segments are annotated: a token which is the begin of a new discourse segment is labelled with `BeginSeg=Yes`. In the remaining three datasets, the full discourse connective is annotated: a token which is the begin of a new discourse segment/connective is labelled with `Seg=B-Conn` and subsequent tokens that are part of the connective are labelled with `Seg=I-Conn`. The task for both annotation schemes is to identify the starts of discourse segments/connectives. In addition, the full connective should be identified for the latter scheme.

Five datasets are only made available in a delexicalised format to participants without a Linguistic Data Consortium membership.

3 Universal Morphosyntactic Features

The following subsections briefly describe how distinct syntactic units are represented in UDG and what features are extracted for the shared task.

3.1 Clauses

Clauses can be extracted from a UDG tree by "cutting" specific clause-marking DepRels. These are: `root`, `csubj`, `ccomp`, `xcomp`, `acl`, `advcl`, `parataxis`, `list`, `vocative` and `discourse`, as well as `conj` if its head is itself governed by a clause-marking DepRel (cf. Dönicke, 2020).[1] Figure 1 shows an example sentence with three clauses, governed by `discourse`, `root` and `xcomp`, respectively. The first two clauses are the starts of a new discourse segment. We handle punctuation at clause boundaries separately. In the example, the comma (,) and the period (.) are stored as preceding and succeeding punctuation of the clause *I 'll try*.

From a clause, we extract the following features: root token's DepRel and POS tag; preceding punctuation; succeeding punctuation.

3.2 NPs

Noun phrases (NPs) realise grammatical roles within a clause. Like clauses, they can be extracted from a UDG tree by cutting specific DepRels. These are: `nsubj`, `obj`, `iobj`, `obl` and `nmod`. In Figure 1, the second clause contains the subject NP *I*, and the third clause contains the object NP *an email*. The **morphological feature structure** (MFS) for each individual word (as given in the data) is shown in (1) and (2), respectively.

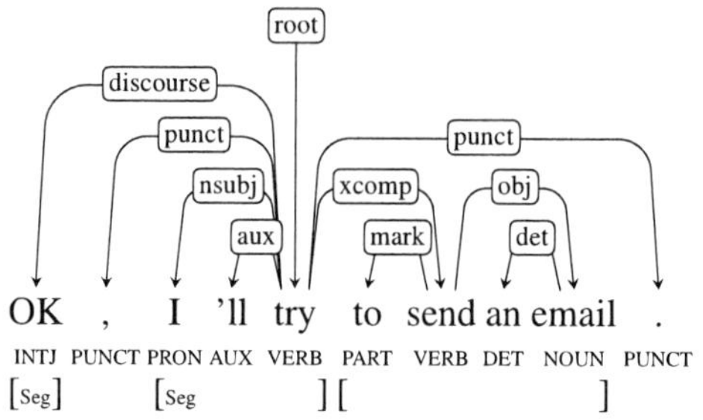

Figure 1: Example sentence from `eng.sdrt.stac`'s development set. Brackets indicate clause spans. All extracted features are shown in Appendix A.

$$\begin{bmatrix} \text{CASE} & \text{Nom} \\ \text{NUMBER} & \text{Sing} \\ \text{PERSON} & 1 \\ \text{PRONTYPE} & \text{Prs} \end{bmatrix} \quad (1)$$

$$\begin{bmatrix} \text{DEFINITE} & \text{Ind} \\ \text{PRONTYPE} & \text{Art} \end{bmatrix} \begin{bmatrix} \text{NUMBER} & \text{Sing} \end{bmatrix} \quad (2)$$

NP-level features are obtained by unifying the MFSs of the involved words into a single feature structure. As a grammatical rule, Case, Person, Number and Gender have to agree for all words within an NP. Sometimes, this rule is violated (in the data) by compound nouns like *internet problems* where the nouns differ in Number (singular vs. plural). Therefore, we take the agreement features only from the NP's root token; all other features are taken from all words (and are allowed to have multiple values). For a proper handling of analytic languages such as Chinese, which tend to mark features not by morphemes but by particles, we introduce a rule for particles that we apply to an NP's root token w before unifying features:

Particle Rule If w has any particles (i.e. dependents with the POS tag PART), move all particles' features to w and delete the particles.

In Figure 2, for example, the particle *de* [的] has the feature $\begin{bmatrix} \text{CASE} & \text{Gen} \end{bmatrix}$, which is moved to the governing noun *lèixíng* [类型].

[1] If the head of a clause-marking DepRel is a modal verb, we do not consider its subtree as a clause because we do not want to separate modal verbs from the verbs they modify; in some treebanks, the modal verb governs the modified verb with an `xcomp` relation (whereas in the English treebanks, the modified verb governs the modal verb with an `aux` relation).

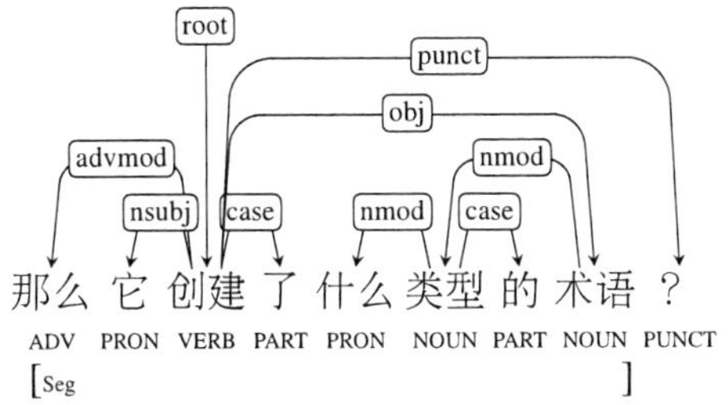

Figure 2: Example sentence from `zho.rst.sctb`'s training set.

From each NP in a clause, we extract: root token's DepRel and POS tag; agreement features: Case, Person, Number, Gender; other nominal features: Degree, Definite, Animacy; lexical features: PronType, NumType, Poss, Reflex, Foreign, Abbr, Typo.[2] To make the features NP-specific, we prefix every feature with the root relation, e.g. $\left[\text{NSUBJ\_CASE} \quad \text{Nom}\right]$, assuming that a clause usually contains only one NP per DepRel.

3.3 Composite Verbs

The composite verb in a clause consists of the main verb and its accompanying full, light, auxiliary and modal verbs as well as verbal particles. (Since we do not distinguish a simple verb form (e.g. *try*) from a compound verb form (e.g. *will try*), we use the term "composite verb" for all cases.) In UDG, we define these as tokens with the POS tag VERB or AUX and subordinate tokens with the POS tag PART and/or the DepRel `compound`. In Figure 1, the second clause contains the composite verb *'ll try*, and the third clause contains the composite verb *to send*. The MFSs of *'ll try* (as given in the data) are shown in (3).

$$\left[\text{VERBFORM} \quad \text{Fin}\right] \left[\text{VERBFORM} \quad \text{Inf}\right] \tag{3}$$

Unfortunately, MFs in the datasets are far from complete; the verbs in (3) are only labelled with VerbForm but not with the other verbal features: Aspect, Mood, Tense, Voice.—An issue that we will take up again in Section 4. For the sake of illustration, we now assume that the MFs are complete, as shown in (4). Note that English finite verbs do not mark Aspect and Voice at the morphological level and English infinitives do not have any inflectional features (both properties differ in other languages).

$$\begin{bmatrix} \text{TENSE} & \text{Pres} \\ \text{MOOD} & \text{Ind} \\ \text{VERBFORM} & \text{Fin} \end{bmatrix} \left[\text{VERBFORM} \quad \text{Inf}\right] \tag{4}$$

Combining the MFSs of the individual words into a single feature structure is not as easily possible as for NPs since there are no linguistic unification/agreement rules amongst the words in a composite verb as they exist for NPs. A simple method for feature extraction would still be to use MFs and prefix them by the POS tag of the corresponding word (and allowing multiple values if there are more than one words with the same POS tag). The **morphosyntactic feature structure** (MSFS) resulting from (4) is shown in (5).

$$\begin{bmatrix} \text{AUX\_MOOD} & \text{Ind} \\ \text{AUX\_TENSE} & \text{Pres} \\ \text{AUX\_VERBFORM} & \text{Fin} \\ \text{VERB\_VERBFORM} & \text{Inf} \end{bmatrix} \tag{5}$$

However, grammaticalised composite verb constructions are quite different for the languages of the world (and also for those in the shared task). Another way to represent (4) is as the **grammatical feature structure** (GFS) in (6).

$$\begin{bmatrix} \text{ASPECT} & \text{Imp} \\ \text{MOOD} & \text{Ind} \\ \text{TENSE} & \text{Fut} \\ \text{VERBFORM} & \text{Fin} \\ \text{VOICE} & \text{Act} \end{bmatrix} \tag{6}$$

Arriving at grammatical features (GFs) is a complex task on its own, which is why we describe the procedure separately in Section 4. Note that the structure in (6) includes $\left[\text{TENSE} \quad \text{Fut}\right]$, since *will try* is grammatically future tense, whereas (5) only includes $\left[\text{AUX\_TENSE} \quad \text{Pres}\right]$ because of the morphological present tense of *will*. GFs assimilate universal clause representations in such that they encode *which* features are expressed by a composite verb and not *how* the verbs are composed. For example, most languages have grammatical future tense, but in some languages (e.g. English) future tense is only marked grammatically whereas in others (e.g. Basque) it is also marked morphologically. We thus assume that GFSs show a greater similarity between languages than MSFSs. Note, however, that GFSs still exhibit differences between languages, because not all languages have parallel grammaticalised constructions.[3]

[2] Explanations and possible values for all of these features can be found at https://universaldependencies.org/u/feat/.

[3] Just to give an example: English has progressive aspect which German has not. The same holds for NPs: German has dative case which English has not.

3.4 Free Discourse Elements

Some words are neither part of an NP nor of the composite verb. If these words are clause-level, i.e. directly governed by the clause's root token, we call them "free discourse elements". These elements comprise e.g. adverbs, complementisers and conjunctions, and are thus very interesting for the task of discourse segmentation. Therefore, we extract DepRel and POS tag from every free discourse element. As for NP-level features, we prefix every feature with the element's DepRel, e.g. $\left[\text{MARK\_POS} \quad \text{SCONJ}\right]$.

3.5 Feature Vectors

When vectorising a document $D = [c_1, \ldots, c_n]$, we get clause vectors $\vec{c}_1, \ldots, \vec{c}_n$, which we then concatenate to context-sensitive vectors $X_D = [\vec{x}_1, \ldots, \vec{x}_n]$ using a window of 3 clauses: $\vec{x}_i = \vec{c}_{i-1} \circ \vec{c}_i \circ \vec{c}_{i+1}$. For the context clauses c_{i-1} and c_{i+1}, we add additional features that indicate whether the clause is in the same sentence as c_i and whether the clause is directly subordinate or directly superordinate to c_i. The classes corresponding to X_D are $Y_D = [y_1, \ldots, y_n]$ with $y_i \in \{\text{TRUE}, \text{FALSE}\}$ (see Section 5.1).

For the documents that include discourse connectives, we create additional vectors $X_D^{Conn} = [\vec{d}_1, \ldots, \vec{d}_m]$ for the connectives $d_1, \ldots, d_m$. Let c_j be the clause that starts with d_j. To construct $\vec{d}_j$, we extract from the first 5 tokens of c_j: POS tag; DepRel; index (starting at 1) of head if the head is among the first five tokens, 0 otherwise. (All features are index-specific, e.g. $\left[\text{1\_POS} \quad \text{INTJ}\right]$.) Since not every clause contains 5 or more tokens, we further add a feature with value $\min\{|c_j|, 5\}$.[4] We will use these features to predict the length of the discourse connectives $Y_D^{Conn} = [|d_1|, \ldots, |d_m|]$ (see Section 5.2).

4 Grammatical TMVM Tagging

Dönicke (2020) presents an algorithm for tagging the GFs Tense, Aspect, Mood, Voice and Modality (TMVM) of a clause in German. The algorithm identifies the words that contribute to a composite verb and uses a function R that maps a bag of MFSs to a GFS, like

$$R\left(\left\{\begin{bmatrix}\text{LEMMA} & \textit{will} \\ \text{TENSE} & \text{Pres} \\ \text{MOOD} & \text{Ind} \\ \text{VERBFORM} & \text{Fin}\end{bmatrix}, \begin{bmatrix}\text{VERBFORM} & \text{Inf}\end{bmatrix}\right\}\right)$$

$$= \begin{bmatrix}\text{ASPECT} & \text{Imp} \\ \text{MOOD} & \text{Ind} \\ \text{TENSE} & \text{Fut} \\ \text{VERBFORM} & \text{Fin} \\ \text{VOICE} & \text{Act}\end{bmatrix},$$

where R relies on a comprehensive table of all composite verb constructions (i.e. the complete conjugation table of the language). Note that only the lemmas of auxiliary verbs are relevant for the algorithm since R does not depend on the main verb. In addition to a list of auxiliary verbs, a list of modal verbs is required.[5]

Algorithm 1 shows an updated version of the original algorithm that has been modified to work with a broader range of languages, specifically the languages in the shared task. In the following, the algorithm is briefly described, with a focus on the adaptions made for multiple languages (numbers in parentheses refer to lines in the pseudocode); for further explanations see Dönicke (2020).

Given a composite verb $V = [v_1, \ldots, v_{|V|}]$ in a language ℓ, first of all the particle rule from Section 3.2 is applied to all words (ll. 1–2). Considering the Chinese example in Figure 2 again, this moves the feature $\left[\text{ASPECT} \quad \text{Perf}\right]$ from the particle *le* [了] to its governing verb *chuàngjiàn* [创建] and removes the particle from V. After this step, V contains only verbs.[6]

The algorithm is designed for an OV language, i.e. a language in which the basic order of object (O) and verb (V) is O-V. More importantly for the algorithm, the basic order of auxiliary (Aux) and verb in OV languages is V-Aux, whereas it is Aux-V in VO languages (Dryer, 1992). Thus, if the input language ℓ is a VO language (see Table 1), V has to be reversed before going on (ll. 3–4).

To counteract finite-verb movement in some languages (e.g. German and Dutch), finite verbs and non-finite verbs are selected separately (ll. 5–6) and then the finite verb is inserted at the syntactically highest position (ll. 7–9). After this step, all verbs in V should be ordered from syntactically lowest

[4] 0.3% of the discourse segments start with a connective that is longer than 5 tokens. These connectives are ignored.

[5] The algorithm differentiates between full verbs, auxiliary verbs and modal verbs. However, UDG only distinguishes full verbs (VERB) and auxiliary verbs (AUX), and modal verbs are tagged as either, depending on the language (see https://universaldependencies.org/u/pos/AUX_.html). Therefore, a list of modal verbs is required to identify them. As a reviewer pointed out, one could also use the language-specific POS tags to identify modal verbs. In our implementation, we also need the lemmas for modal unification across languages (see text).

[6] As in linguistic works (e.g. Antonenko, 2008; Dobrushina, 2012), we also consider the Russian бы as particle although it is tagged with AUX in the Russian dataset.

Algorithm 1: Compute features of composite verb V in language ℓ

```
1  for i = 1 to |V| do
2      particle_rule(v_i)
3  if ℓ is VO language then
4      V ← [v_|V|, ..., v_1]
5  V_fin ← [finite verbs in V]
6  V ← [non-finite verbs in V]
7  if |V_fin| > 0 then
8      v_fin ← right-most finite verb in V_fin
9      V ← [v_1, ..., v_|V|, v_fin]
10 if |V| = 0 then
11     return [ ]
12 else if main verb in V then
13     v_main ← right-most main verb in V
14 else
15     v_main ← left-most verb in V
16 V ← [v_main, ..., v_fin]
17 M ← [features*(v_i, ℓ) for i = 1 to |V|]
18 for i = |V| to 1 do
19     if v_i is modal verb then
20         m_{i-1} ← m_i
21 while |V| > 0 do
22     Set v_1 to be the main verb
23     F ←      X           m_{|M|-|V|+i}
            1≤i≤|V|
      v_i is not modal verb
24     if Σ_{i=1}^{|F|} Σ_{j=1}^{|f_i|} |f_ij| = 0 then
25         return [ ]
26     A ← {}
27     for i = 1 to |F| do
28         A ∪← R*(f_i, ℓ)
29     if |A| = 0 ∧ |V| = 1 then
30         A ← m_|M|
31     if |A| > 0 then
32         A ← filter(A)
33         a ← combine(A)
34         a ← unify_verb_form(a)
35         V_modal ← [modal verbs in V]
36         V_modal ← unify_modals(V_modal, ℓ)
37         a ⊔← [MODALITY  V_modal]
38         return a
39     V ← [v_2, ..., v_|V|]
40 return [ ]
```

$\overset{\cup}{\leftarrow}$ and $\overset{\sqcup}{\leftarrow}$ are augmented assignment operators for union and unification, respectively.

to highest position.

If V is not empty (ll. 10–11), the main verb is determined (ll. 12–15) and all syntactically lower verbs are removed from V (l. 16), because they are not relevant for TMVM tagging.

The MFs of each $v_i \in V$ are stored in $m_i \in M$ (l. 17), where m_i is a set of MFSs since it is (theoretically) possible that a verb is morphologically ambiguous. However, since the MFs for each verb are given in the data, $|m_i| = 1$ per default.[7,8]

As in the original algorithm, MFs of modal verbs overwrite those of syntactically lower verbs (ll. 18–20). All possible combinations of the involved verbs' MFSs, excluding modal verbs, are then stored in $F = \{f_1, \ldots, f_{|F|}\}$ (l. 23). In a simple case with no modal verbs and $|m_i| = 1$ for all $m_i \in M$, $|F| = 1$ and f_1 contains the MFS of every verb $v_1, \ldots, v_{|V|}$, i.e. $f_1 = \{m_{11}, \ldots, m_{|V|_1}\}$.[9]

Every combination $f_i \in F$ is then analysed with the language-specific look-up table and the analyses (i.e. GFSs) are stored in A (ll. 26–28).[10] As mentioned in Section 3.3, a lot of MFs are missing in the data. R^* treats missing features as features with wildcard values and returns all matching analyses, which means that the number of returned analyses for f_i increases with the number of missing features in each $f_{i_j} \in f_i$ and would become maximal if every f_{i_j} is empty. As a basic restriction, we require that at least one f_{i_j} is not empty and return an empty feature structure otherwise (ll. 24–25).

In contrast to too many analyses, it is also possible that no analysis is found. In this case, the syntactically lowest verb is removed (l. 39) and the look-up is repeated (l. 21). If only one verb is left and still no analysis is found, A is set to the verb's MFSs (ll. 29–30).

The analyses in A are then filtered (l. 32), e.g. by giving higher preference to analyses with

[7]As in Dönicke (2020), we add the participle analysis to potential substitute infinitives in German.

[8]We perform a small number of modifications to the MFs for cases where we think that the data is not labelled ideally. For example, some languages use $\left[\text{VERBFORM} \quad \text{Ger}\right]$ and some use $\begin{bmatrix}\text{TENSE} & \text{Pres} \\ \text{VERBFORM} & \text{Part}\end{bmatrix}$ for very similar forms of the verb (gerunds and present participles). For this reason, the UD guidelines discourage the use of $\left[\text{VERBFORM} \quad \text{Ger}\right]$ (see https://universaldependencies.org/u/feat/VerbForm.html#Ger) and we convert it to the latter feature combination.

[9]Actually, the Cartesian product yields an ordered combination $[m_{11}, \ldots, m_{|V|_1}]$ but we treat it as unordered combination to be less prone to potential local verb movements.

[10]The look-up tables have been created manually. For some languages, this required extensive study of composite verb constructions, and we want to acknowledge a few works that were very helpful in this process: Berro et al. (2019) for Basque, Izadi and Rahimi (2015) for Persian, Babby and Brecht (1975) for Russian, Jendraschek (2011) for Turkish, and Li and Thompson (1989) for Chinese.

[VOICE Act] and/or [MOOD Ind]. The remaining analyses are unified into a single GFS a, ignoring features with conflicting values (l. 33).

Since not all languages have the same types of non-finite verb forms, we normalise them as follows (l. 34):

$$\begin{aligned}
[\text{VERBFORM} \ \ \text{Inf}] \sqsubseteq a : a \leftarrow \begin{bmatrix} \text{VERBFORM} & \text{Inf} \\ \text{VERBFORM*} & \text{Verb} \end{bmatrix} \\
[\text{VERBFORM} \ \ \text{Vnoun}] \sqsubseteq a : a \leftarrow \begin{bmatrix} \text{VERBFORM} & \text{Inf} \\ \text{VERBFORM*} & \text{Noun} \end{bmatrix} \\
[\text{VERBFORM} \ \ \text{Part}] \sqsubseteq a : a \leftarrow \begin{bmatrix} \text{VERBFORM} & \text{Part} \\ \text{VERBFORM*} & \text{Adj} \end{bmatrix} \\
[\text{VERBFORM} \ \ \text{Conv}] \sqsubseteq a : a \leftarrow \begin{bmatrix} \text{VERBFORM} & \text{Part} \\ \text{VERBFORM*} & \text{Adv} \end{bmatrix}
\end{aligned}$$

In a last step, we add the modal verbs to a (ll. 35–37). In Dönicke (2020), the lemmas of the verbs are used but in our multilingual implementation, we map the lemmas to three categories of modal verbs (cf. Biber et al., 2002, p. 176): permission/possibility/ability (POS), obligation/necessity (OBL), and volition/prediction (VOL).

5 Classification

We expect a high interdependence between the extracted features, which is why we use decision trees for the classification of clauses. A decision tree is a statistical classification method that can both learn such complex dependencies and also visualise them in an understandable manner.

Experiments with other classifiers, including complement Naive Bayes, random forest and multilayer perceptron, could not improve the performance over that of a simple decision tree. This suggests that the decision tree makes the best out of the available features.

5.1 Discourse Segments

Given a training set $X_{D_{train}}$, we train a decision tree classifier with Gini impurity as split criterion. Since the performance of a decision tree strongly depends on its depth and leaf size, grid search is performed to select the optimal values for the maximum tree depth in $\{5, 10, 15, 20, 25, \infty\}$ and the minimum leaf size in $\{1, 2, 5, 10, 15, 20\}$. For the grid search, the development set $X_{D_{dev}}$ corresponding to $X_{D_{train}}$ is used for validation.

5.2 Discourse Connectives

The classifier that predicts the length of a connective is also a decision tree with Gini impurity as split criterion. We let this tree fully expand on the training set $X^{Conn}_{D_{train}}$ (maximum tree depth = ∞; minimum leaf size = 1) since we assume that discourse connectives are like a closed class and generalising to unseen feature combinations is rarely needed.

6 Experiments

Parsed vs. Plain As suggested in the shared task, we evaluate our systems in two main conditions: using the parsed/treebanked datasets (`.conllu` files) and using the plain/tokenised datasets (`.tok` files). We approach the second condition by preprocessing the plain datasets with spaCy (https://spacy.io/) and training new classifiers on the processed training sets. SpaCy provides pretrained UDG models for all shared task's languages except German, Persian, Basque and Turkish. For these languages, we trained new models on the UD treebanks HDT (German), PerDT (Persian), BDT (Basque) and Kenet (Turkish) (Zeman et al., 2021).

Morphosyntactic vs. Grammatical In all experiments, we represent composite verbs either as morphosyntactic (M) or as grammatical (G) feature structures (as described in Section 3.3).

Monolingual vs. Multilingual Each system is evaluated on all 16 test sets. In the monolingual condition, we train a system on one dataset only. We further train a system on all training sets combined (ALL) as well as 16 systems on all but one training sets (CV). In the CV condition, we evaluate the system on the test set corresponding to the excluded training set. Thus, the CV condition corresponds to a scenario without training data for the test language.

7 Results and Discussion

Tables 2 and 3 show the results in the parsed and the plain condition. Numbers are the F1 scores for discourse segmentation or connective identification, depending on the dataset. For the monolingual experiments, the highest value in each column is boldfaced. For the multilingual experiments, the higher value on each test set is underlined. In the monolingual experiments, the F1 scores for parsed data are on average 3.5% higher than those for plain data. The best result on a test set is usually achieved by the system trained on the corresponding training set.

The systems presented in this paper do not perform better than the best systems from DISRPT

Training set	Test set: deu.rst.pcc		eng.pdtb.pdtb		eng.rst.gum		eng.rst.rstdt		eng.sdrt.stac		eus.rst.ert		fas.rst.prstc		fra.sdrt.annodis		nld.rst.nldt		por.rst.cstn		rus.rst.rrt		spa.rst.rststb		spa.rst.sctb		tur.pdtb.tdb		zho.pdtb.cdtb		zho.rst.sctb	
	M	G	M	G	M	G	M	G	M	G	M	G	M	G	M	G	M	G	M	G	M	G	M	G	M	G	M	G	M	G	M	G
deu.rst.pcc	**89**	**92**	26	25	73	76	66	62	91	91	71	71	66	63	57	58	87	89	67	72	64	65	80	78	65	63	7	7	18	18	63	65
eng.pdtb.pdtb	29	27	**74**	**74**	29	29	25	21	8	8	25	25	20	21	13	14	22	21	22	21	24	24	25	26	16	15	13	16	7	10	7	8
eng.rst.gum	88	89	26	28	**86**	**86**	**80**	**80**	89	89	69	70	74	73	60	61	85	85	74	74	67	67	74	74	57	57	6	6	19	**21**	52	55
eng.rst.rstdt	86	87	26	26	83	83	75	75	88	88	69	70	75	69	61	61	83	83	73	72	63	65	70	72	55	55	6	6	19	19	43	48
eng.sdrt.stac	85	85	21	21	64	64	51	51	**92**	**92**	70	70	61	61	50	50	82	82	64	64	59	59	77	77	68	68	8	8	16	16	73	**73**
eus.rst.ert	86	86	28	27	65	66	55	53	91	90	**73**	**75**	64	62	52	52	85	86	67	65	65	64	80	80	67	67	12	9	17	17	**74**	69
fas.rst.prstc	87	88	34	32	72	73	64	68	91	90	**73**	71	**80**	**81**	54	56	83	83	68	70	67	67	74	77	61	62	7	8	**20**	19	68	65
fra.sdrt.annodis	87	87	27	32	76	78	55	71	72	88	69	70	70	71	**62**	**62**	85	86	73	73	66	66	75	76	58	59	7	7	16	18	72	53
nld.rst.nldt	87	87	32	35	74	73	58	57	91	90	72	74	67	67	55	57	**90**	**90**	73	69	68	67	83	83	66	64	11	12	17	17	64	72
por.rst.cstn	88	86	30	33	76	73	59	23	90	59	69	69	63	65	60	57	85	84	**80**	**80**	67	66	78	76	62	60	10	7	18	3	59	56
rus.rst.rrt	**89**	89	26	26	69	70	55	54	85	86	71	70	62	66	55	55	86	87	71	71	**73**	**73**	78	79	63	64	9	9	17	16	68	68
spa.rst.rststb	87	87	30	32	69	70	54	54	83	83	69	69	56	58	54	52	79	83	70	69	66	66	**86**	**85**	**69**	**69**	8	7	16	16	62	62
spa.rst.sctb	78	85	20	27	60	67	51	51	81	89	65	68	56	19	48	48	76	80	63	65	59	60	79	78	65	66	8	7	16	16	73	39
tur.pdtb.tdb	5	7	30	33	11	14	8	8	1	1	10	10	9	14	8	8	9	12	14	15	12	14	11	12	10	10	**37**	**37**	1	1	2	2
zho.pdtb.cdtb	0	0	1	1	0	0	0	0	0	0	1	1	1	1	1	1	0	0	0	0	0	0	0	0	0	0	0	0	2	2	0	0
zho.rst.sctb	69	69	17	17	53	53	47	47	65	65	64	64	53	53	46	46	72	72	54	54	56	56	73	73	62	62	9	9	15	15	72	72
ALL	89	89	72	71	77	77	26	20	91	91	73	73	76	76	59	58	89	88	76	76	72	73	84	84	65	67	34	33	8	10	70	68
CV	90	90	26	26	71	70	24	19	81	83	72	71	67	63	58	57	88	87	74	74	65	66	81	80	66	66	13	13	5	13	65	62

Table 2: Results on the parsed data in %.

Training set	Test set: deu.rst.pcc		eng.pdtb.pdtb		eng.rst.gum		eng.rst.rstdt		eng.sdrt.stac		eus.rst.ert		fas.rst.prstc		fra.sdrt.annodis		nld.rst.nldt		por.rst.cstn		rus.rst.rrt		spa.rst.rststb		spa.rst.sctb		tur.pdtb.tdb		zho.pdtb.cdtb		zho.rst.sctb	
	M	G	M	G	M	G	M	G	M	G	M	G	M	G	M	G	M	G	M	G	M	G	M	G	M	G	M	G	M	G	M	G
deu.rst.pcc	**89**	**89**	–	–	–	–	–	–	53	53	69	69	71	71	57	56	82	81	67	67	62	62	71	73	63	63	–	–	–	–	65	64
eng.pdtb.pdtb	–	–	*48*	*48*	–	–	–	–	–	–	–	–	–	–	–	–	–	–	–	–	–	–	–	–	–	–	–	–	–	–	–	–
eng.rst.gum	–	–	–	–	*75*	*75*	–	–	–	–	–	–	–	–	–	–	–	–	–	–	–	–	–	–	–	–	–	–	–	–	–	–
eng.rst.rstdt	–	–	–	–	–	–	*80*	*80*	–	–	–	–	–	–	–	–	–	–	–	–	–	–	–	–	–	–	–	–	–	–	–	–
eng.sdrt.stac	78	83	–	–	–	–	–	–	**67**	**69**	60	62	62	71	55	62	79	81	68	72	58	58	72	70	59	57	–	–	–	–	55	48
eus.rst.ert	83	84	–	–	–	–	–	–	51	52	**72**	**73**	55	56	53	53	82	81	63	67	60	59	74	76	69	67	–	–	–	–	69	69
fas.rst.prstc	88	86	–	–	–	–	–	–	57	57	70	69	**77**	**74**	57	56	83	83	67	66	64	63	74	74	63	65	–	–	–	–	67	67
fra.sdrt.annodis	85	85	–	–	–	–	–	–	59	55	65	65	65	64	**66**	**65**	83	83	73	76	64	65	71	72	57	61	–	–	–	–	54	64
nld.rst.nldt	86	85	–	–	–	–	–	–	54	53	71	71	66	64	56	57	**87**	**87**	67	68	64	64	77	77	62	**68**	–	–	–	–	67	**70**
por.rst.cstn	84	85	–	–	–	–	–	–	54	54	68	67	64	61	60	62	84	85	**77**	**77**	65	65	74	72	62	59	–	–	–	–	69	69
rus.rst.rrt	87	87	–	–	–	–	–	–	48	51	70	68	61	65	56	58	80	83	68	72	**71**	**71**	73	73	64	64	–	–	–	–	68	68
spa.rst.rststb	84	82	–	–	–	–	–	–	43	46	68	69	57	64	55	54	79	80	69	68	63	61	**80**	**81**	68	**68**	–	–	–	–	**70**	**70**
spa.rst.sctb	85	82	–	–	–	–	–	–	51	46	65	65	59	59	53	53	81	77	64	63	60	55	77	78	**69**	**68**	–	–	–	–	**70**	**70**
tur.pdtb.tdb	–	–	–	–	–	–	–	–	–	–	–	–	–	–	–	–	–	–	–	–	–	–	–	–	–	–	*41*	*41*	–	–	–	–
zho.pdtb.cdtb	–	–	–	–	–	–	–	–	–	–	–	–	–	–	–	–	–	–	–	–	–	–	–	–	–	–	–	–	*9*	*9*	–	–
zho.rst.sctb	80	80	–	–	–	–	–	–	50	50	63	63	56	56	45	45	77	77	59	59	55	55	71	71	68	**68**	–	–	–	–	69	69
ALL	86	88	–	–	–	–	–	–	65	65	72	72	73	74	61	62	84	85	75	75	71	71	80	79	67	65	–	–	–	–	67	69
CV	85	87	–	–	–	–	–	–	49	51	70	70	63	63	61	59	84	83	72	73	65	65	76	78	68	65	–	–	–	–	65	65

Table 3: Results on the plain data in %. Delexicalised datasets are excluded because they cannot be preprocessed; italicised results have been obtained by the shared task organisers.

2019 (Zeldes et al., 2019). A fundamental difference between previous systems and the current system is the classification approach: Whereas previous works performed a token-level classification, the current work tries a clause-level classification. The latter approach relies on the assumption that starts of discourse segments are almost always starts of clauses; and it was our mistake and maybe also bit of an unfortunate coincidence that we checked this hypothesis only for `deu.rst.pcc` and `eng.sdrt.stac` (the datasets which we mostly used for development), where indeed 95% and 97%, respectively, of the segment starts coincide with clause starts. As we can see in Table 4, the percentage is much lower in other datasets. Since we train our decision tree to

Dataset	%	R	P	F1	$F1_1^*$	$F1_2^*$
discourse segmentation						
deu.rst.pcc	95	89	95	92	94	–
eng.rst.gum	85	80	94	86	94	–
eng.rst.rstdt	84	66	87	75	80	–
eng.sdrt.stac	97	86	99	92	94	–
eus.rst.ert	85	66	87	75	84	–
fas.rst.prstc	80	74	88	81	91	–
fra.sdrt.annodis	65	50	82	62	83	–
nld.rst.nldt	93	86	95	90	95	–
por.rst.cstn	74	68	97	80	95	–
rus.rst.rrt	82	64	86	73	85	–
spa.rst.rststb	91	82	89	85	90	–
spa.rst.sctb	88	57	79	66	79	–
zho.rst.sctb	88	67	79	72	81	–
mean	85	72	89	79	88	–
connective identification						
eng.pdtb.pdtb	82	66	86	74	84	97
tur.pdtb.tdb	44	24	80	37	63	96
zho.pdtb.cdtb	40	1	30	2	6	89
mean	55	30	65	38	51	94

Table 4: Percentage of segment starts that are also clause starts, and achieved recall, precision and F1 (see Table 2) for each dataset. $F1_1^*$ and $F1_2^*$ are the F1 scores of the individual classifiers that predict clause-initial segment starts and connective lengths, respectively.

distinguish clauses where the first token is the start of a discourse segment from all other clauses (including clauses that contain starts of discourse segments at non-initial positions), the percentage sets an upper bound for the classification recall. The languages with the highest achieved precision are English (86%–99%), Portuguese (97%), German (95%) and Dutch (95%); the languages with the highest F1 are German (92%), English (74%–92%) and Dutch (90%). If only clause-initial segment starts are taken into account ($F1_1^*$ in Table 4), the F1 of the decision tree significantly increases for almost all datasets (+9% on average). The performance for determining the length of discourse connectives ranges between 89% and 97% ($F2_1^*$ in Table 4).

These results suggest that the clause-level approach could achieve reasonable results if segment starts would always coincide with clause starts. This precondition is, however, hard to fulfil, since there are not only different frameworks for discourse segmentation but also different notions of what a clause is. In this paper, we define clauses in terms of UDG. In practice, UD annotations are carried out by many different research groups or converted from non-UD treebanks and thus prone to inconsistencies that may also affect the annotations of clause-marking relations (e.g. de Marneffe et al., 2017). Furthermore, a lot of the datasets in the shared task incorporate automatically created dependency trees (created by models trained on UD treebanks), which may lead to follow-up errors in the clause-splitting step. Dönicke (2020) reports an F1 of 81% for predicting clauses in a German text after preprocessing it with a spaCy model trained on the German UD treebanks. Even though this number only gives a rough estimate on how well our system identifies clauses, there is clearly room for improvement. One could also try to resolve the mismatch between segment starts and clause starts in a postprocessing step, e.g. by a second classifier that identifies the position of a segment start in a clause (similar to our connective-length classifier).

All of the systems from DISRPT 2019 use lexical features, where the best systems (Muller et al., 2019; Iruskieta et al., 2019) are recurrent neural networks. The system that is most similar to the current work is the (best) system from Bourgonje and Schäfer (2019), who use a random forest classifier and extract features at the token-level, e.g. surface form, POS tag, position in the sentence, succeeding punctuation mark. Like we do with clauses, they extract features from the current, the preceding and the succeeding token. For German and Basque, our clause-level, delexicalised and unordered-tree approach yields higher F1s than Bourgonje and Schäfer (2019)'s random forest; these are, however, the only languages on which our system performs better. The motivation for not using lexical features was to create language-independent, universal representations for multilingual learning. However, lexical features potentially improve the performance in a monolingual setting.[11]

[11] A multilingual alternative to lexical features are semantic features, which we also experimented with in the development phase. We extracted semantic features for English verbs and their synonyms in the other languages from ConceptNet (Speer et al., 2017), and added the features of a clause's main verb to its grammatical feature structure. (The most common semantic features are: change, contact, communication, motion, social, stative, possession, cognition, body, creation, perception, emotion.) Using these features could not improve our results. A possible reason for this is that we assigned semantic features without disambiguating verb senses and therefore a lot of verbs received a broad range of features. However, we are not aware of an existing multilingual resource for word

Training on all languages does never improve over the performance of the best monolingual system. The results with a multilingual training set, however, might be distorted because `eng.pdtb.pdtb`, `tur.pdtb.tdb` and `rus.rst.rrt` constitute far larger parts in the multilingual training set than the other datasets. This is also visible in the CV experiments: when one of the large datasets is excluded, the performance drops more than when a smaller dataset is excluded. For example, the performance drops from 71% to 26% when `eng.pdtb.pdtb` is excluded, whereas it drops from 67% to 66% when `spa.rst.sctb` (the smallest dataset) is excluded. Although our system does not profit from multilingual training in the context of the shared task, it might be useful in scenarios where no training data is available for a language. For example, training and testing on `spa.rst.rststb` achieves an F1 of 85%, and training on other RST treebanks leads to 72%–83% on `spa.rst.rststb` (see Table 2). Note that training on the small but same-language treebank `spa.rst.sctb` yields 78%, whereas training on `nld.rst.nldt`, which is three times as large, yields 83%. Joining only some and not all datasets might improve the performance for individual languages as well. Future work on multilingual training could also experiment with balanced datasets.

The use of GFSs instead of MSFSs did not have a great impact on the classification performance (<1% difference on average). Inspection of the learned decision trees showed that the top-level features concern punctuation, clause types, free discourse elements and partially NPs, but features concerning the verb are less common. (As an extreme example, the decision tree for `eng.sdrt.stac`, see Appendix B, does not include any verbal feature.) Unexpectedly, tense, mood, voice etc. seem to be irrelevant for discourse segmentation, and so it does not matter how they are represented.

8 Conclusion

In this paper, we approached discourse segmentation as a clause-level classification task and represented clauses as delexicalised UD-based feature structures. While the approach works sufficiently on some datasets (e.g. German), the performance is generally lower than that of other approaches (cf. Zeldes et al., 2019). A major reason for this is that, contrary to our expectation, boundaries of discourse segments do not typically fall onto clause boundaries in most datasets.

In the context of the shared task, we extended Dönicke (2020)'s algorithm for the grammatical analysis of composite verb forms and created the language-specific resources to run it for all 11 languages. Thus, we also contribute to the task of compound-verb analysis, which is (in contrast to morphological analysis) underrepresented in NLP.[12] However, annotating data with grammatical features and testing the algorithm goes beyond the scope of participating in the shared task and is left to future work.

Our system is available at https://gitlab.gwdg.de/tillmann.doenicke/disrpt2021-tmvm.

sense disambiguation and semantic feature assignment.

[12] We are aware of works on Czech (Žáčková et al., 2000), Hindi (Choudhary et al., 2014), Italian (Faro and Pavone, 2015), German, French and English (Ramm et al., 2017; Myers and Palmer, 2019).

References

Andrei Antonenko. 2008. The nature of Russian subjunctive clauses.

Leonard H. Babby and Richard D. Brecht. 1975. The syntax of voice in Russian. *Language*, 51(2):342–367.

Ane Berro, Fernández Beatriz, and Jon Ortiz de Urbina, editors. 2019. *Basque and Romance: Aligning Grammars*. Grammars and Sketches of the World's Languages. Brill.

Douglas Biber, Stig Johansson, Geoffrey Leech, Susan Conrad, and Edward Finegan. 2002. *Longman grammar of spoken and written English*. Second impression 2003.

Peter Bourgonje and Robin Schäfer. 2019. Multilingual and cross-genre discourse unit segmentation. In *Proceedings of the Workshop on Discourse Relation Parsing and Treebanking 2019*, pages 105–114, Minneapolis, MN. Association for Computational Linguistics.

Narayan Choudhary, Pramod Pandey, and Girish Nath Jha. 2014. A rule based method for the identification of TAM features in a PoS tagged corpus. In *Human Language Technology Challenges for Computer Science and Linguistics*, pages 178–188, Cham. Springer International Publishing.

Marie-Catherine de Marneffe, Matias Grioni, Jenna Kanerva, and Filip Ginter. 2017. Assessing the annotation consistency of the Universal Dependencies corpora. In *Proceedings of the Fourth International Conference on Dependency Linguistics (Depling 2017)*, pages 108–115, Pisa,Italy. Linköping University Electronic Press.

Liesbeth Degand and Anne Catherine Simon. 2009. On identifying basic discourse units in speech: theoretical and empirical issues. *Discours* [En ligne], 4.

Nina Dobrushina. 2012. Subjunctive complement clauses in Russian. *Russian linguistics*, 36(2):121–156.

Tillmann Dönicke. 2020. Clause-level tense, mood, voice and modality tagging for German. In *Proceedings of the 19th International Workshop on Treebanks and Linguistic Theories*, pages 1–17, Düsseldorf, Germany. Association for Computational Linguistics.

Matthew S. Dryer. 1992. The Greenbergian word order correlations. *Language*, 68:81–138.

Simone Faro and Arianna Pavone. 2015. Refined tagging of complex verbal phrases for the Italian language. In *Proceedings of the Prague Stringology Conference 2015*, pages 132–145, Czech Technical University in Prague, Czech Republic.

Mikel Iruskieta, Kepa Bengoetxea, Aitziber Atutxa Salazar, and Arantza Diaz de Ilarraza. 2019. Multilingual segmentation based on neural networks and pre-trained word embeddings. In *Proceedings of the Workshop on Discourse Relation Parsing and Treebanking 2019*, pages 125–132, Minneapolis, MN. Association for Computational Linguistics.

Mehri Izadi and Maryam Rahimi. 2015. Word order of Persian and English: A processing-based analysis. *Education Journal*, 4(1):37–43.

Gerd Jendraschek. 2011. A fresh look at the tense-aspect system of Turkish. *Language Research*, 47(2):245–270.

Charles N. Li and Sandra A. Thompson. 1989. *Mandarin Chinese: A Functional Reference Grammar*. University of California Press.

William C. Mann and Sandra A. Thompson. 1988. Rhetorical structure theory: Toward a functional theory of text organization. *Text*, 8:243–281.

Philippe Muller, Chloé Braud, and Mathieu Morey. 2019. ToNy: Contextual embeddings for accurate multilingual discourse segmentation of full documents. In *Proceedings of the Workshop on Discourse Relation Parsing and Treebanking 2019*, pages 115–124, Minneapolis, MN. Association for Computational Linguistics.

Skatje Myers and Martha Palmer. 2019. ClearTAC: Verb tense, aspect, and form classification using neural nets. In *Proceedings of the First International Workshop on Designing Meaning Representations*, pages 136–140, Florence, Italy. Association for Computational Linguistics.

Joakim Nivre, Marie-Catherine de Marneffe, Filip Ginter, Yoav Goldberg, Jan Hajič, Christopher D. Manning, Ryan McDonald, Slav Petrov, Sampo Pyysalo, Natalia Silveira, Reut Tsarfaty, and Daniel Zeman. 2016. Universal Dependencies v1: A multilingual treebank collection. In *Proceedings of the Tenth International Conference on Language Resources and Evaluation (LREC'16)*, pages 1659–1666, Portorož, Slovenia. European Language Resources Association (ELRA).

Anita Ramm, Sharid Loáiciga, Annemarie Friedrich, and Alexander Fraser. 2017. Annotating tense, mood and voice for English, French and German. In *Proceedings of ACL 2017, System Demonstrations*, pages 1–6, Vancouver, Canada. Association for Computational Linguistics.

Robyn Speer, Joshua Chin, and Catherine Havasi. 2017. Conceptnet 5.5: An open multilingual graph of general knowledge. In *Thirty-first AAAI conference on artificial intelligence*.

Eva Žáčková, Luboš Popelínský, and Miloslav Nepil. 2000. Automatic tagging of compound verb groups in Czech corpora. In *Text, Speech and Dialogue*, pages 115–120, Berlin, Heidelberg. Springer Berlin Heidelberg.

Amir Zeldes, Debopam Das, Erick Galani Maziero, Juliano Antonio, and Mikel Iruskieta. 2019. The DISRPT 2019 shared task on elementary discourse unit segmentation and connective detection. In *Proceedings of the Workshop on Discourse Relation Parsing and Treebanking 2019*, pages 97–104, Minneapolis, MN. Association for Computational Linguistics.

Daniel Zeman, Joakim Nivre, Mitchell Abrams, Elia Ackermann, Noëmi Aepli, Hamid Aghaei, Željko Agić, Amir Ahmadi, Lars Ahrenberg, Chika Kennedy Ajede, Gabrielė Aleksandravičiūtė, Ika Alfina, Lene Antonsen, Katya Aplonova, Angelina Aquino, Carolina Aragon, Maria Jesus Aranzabe, Bilge Nas Arıcan, Hórunn Arnardóttir, Gashaw Arutie, Jessica Naraiswari Arwidarasti, Masayuki Asahara, Deniz Baran Aslan, Luma Ateyah, Furkan Atmaca, Mohammed Attia, Aitziber Atutxa, Liesbeth Augustinus, Elena Badmaeva, Keerthana Balasubramani, Miguel Ballesteros, Esha Banerjee, Sebastian Bank, Verginica Barbu Mititelu, Starkaður Barkarson, Victoria Basmov, Colin Batchelor, John Bauer, Seyyit Talha Bedir, Kepa Bengoetxea, Gözde Berk, Yevgeni Berzak, Irshad Ahmad Bhat, Riyaz Ahmad Bhat, Erica Biagetti, Eckhard Bick, Agnė Bielinskienė, Kristín Bjarnadóttir, Rogier Blokland, Victoria Bobicev, Loïc Boizou, Emanuel Borges Völker, Carl Börstell, Cristina Bosco, Gosse Bouma, Sam Bowman, Adriane Boyd, Anouck Braggaar, Kristina Brokaitė, Aljoscha Burchardt, Marie Candito, Bernard Caron, Gauthier Caron, Lauren Cassidy, Tatiana Cavalcanti, Gülşen Cebiroğlu Eryiğit, Flavio Massimiliano Cecchini, Giuseppe G. A. Celano, Slavomír Čéplö, Neslihan Cesur, Savas Cetin, Özlem Çetinoğlu,

Fabricio Chalub, Shweta Chauhan, Ethan Chi, Taishi Chika, Yongseok Cho, Jinho Choi, Jayeol Chun, Alessandra T. Cignarella, Silvie Cinková, Aurélie Collomb, Çağrı Çöltekin, Miriam Connor, Marine Courtin, Mihaela Cristescu, Philemon. Daniel, Elizabeth Davidson, Marie-Catherine de Marneffe, Valeria de Paiva, Mehmet Oguz Derin, Elvis de Souza, Arantza Diaz de Ilarraza, Carly Dickerson, Arawinda Dinakaramani, Elisa Di Nuovo, Bamba Dione, Peter Dirix, Kaja Dobrovoljc, Timothy Dozat, Kira Droganova, Puneet Dwivedi, Hanne Eckhoff, Sandra Eiche, Marhaba Eli, Ali Elkahky, Binyam Ephrem, Olga Erina, Tomaž Erjavec, Aline Etienne, Wograine Evelyn, Sidney Facundes, Richárd Farkas, Marília Fernanda, Hector Fernandez Alcalde, Jennifer Foster, Cláudia Freitas, Kazunori Fujita, Katarína Gajdošová, Daniel Galbraith, Marcos Garcia, Moa Gärdenfors, Sebastian Garza, Fabrício Ferraz Gerardi, Kim Gerdes, Filip Ginter, Gustavo Godoy, Iakes Goenaga, Koldo Gojenola, Memduh Gökırmak, Yoav Goldberg, Xavier Gómez Guinovart, Berta González Saavedra, Bernadeta Griciūtė, Matias Grioni, Loïc Grobol, Normunds Grūzītis, Bruno Guillaume, Céline Guillot-Barbance, Tunga Güngör, Nizar Habash, Hinrik Hafsteinsson, Jan Hajič, Jan Hajič jr., Mika Hämäläinen, Linh Hà Mỹ, Na-Rae Han, Muhammad Yudistira Hanifmuti, Sam Hardwick, Kim Harris, Dag Haug, Johannes Heinecke, Oliver Hellwig, Felix Hennig, Barbora Hladká, Jaroslava Hlaváčová, Florinel Hociung, Petter Hohle, Eva Huber, Jena Hwang, Takumi Ikeda, Anton Karl Ingason, Radu Ion, Elena Irimia, Ọlájídé Ishola, Kaoru Ito, Tomáš Jelínek, Apoorva Jha, Anders Johannsen, Hildur Jónsdóttir, Fredrik Jørgensen, Markus Juutinen, Sarveswaran K, Hüner Kaşıkara, Andre Kaasen, Nadezhda Kabaeva, Sylvain Kahane, Hiroshi Kanayama, Jenna Kanerva, Neslihan Kara, Boris Katz, Tolga Kayadelen, Jessica Kenney, Václava Kettnerová, Jesse Kirchner, Elena Klementieva, Arne Köhn, Abdullatif Köksal, Kamil Kopacewicz, Timo Korkiakangas, Natalia Kotsyba, Jolanta Kovalevskaitė, Simon Krek, Parameswari Krishnamurthy, Oğuzhan Kuyrukçu, Aslı Kuzgun, Sookyoung Kwak, Veronika Laippala, Lucia Lam, Lorenzo Lambertino, Tatiana Lando, Septina Dian Larasati, Alexei Lavrentiev, John Lee, Phương Lê Hồng, Alessandro Lenci, Saran Lertpradit, Herman Leung, Maria Levina, Cheuk Ying Li, Josie Li, Keying Li, Yuan Li, Kyung-Tae Lim, Bruna Lima Padovani, Krister Lindén, Nikola Ljubešić, Olga Loginova, Andry Luthfi, Mikko Luukko, Olga Lyashevskaya, Teresa Lynn, Vivien Macketanz, Aibek Makazhanov, Michael Mandl, Christopher Manning, Ruli Manurung, Büşra Marşan, Cătălina Mărănduc, David Mareček, Katrin Marheinecke, Héctor Martínez Alonso, André Martins, Jan Mašek, Hiroshi Matsuda, Yuji Matsumoto, Alessandro Mazzei, Ryan McDonald, Sarah McGuinness, Gustavo Mendonça, Niko Miekka, Karina Mischenkova, Margarita Misirpashayeva, Anna Missilä, Cătălin Mititelu, Maria Mitrofan, Yusuke Miyao, AmirHossein Mojiri Foroushani, Judit Molnár, Amirsaeid Moloodi, Simonetta Montemagni, Amir More, Laura Moreno Romero, Giovanni Moretti, Keiko Sophie Mori, Shinsuke Mori, Tomohiko Morioka, Shigeki Moro, Bjartur Mortensen, Bohdan Moskalevskyi, Kadri Muischnek, Robert Munro, Yugo Murawaki, Kaili Müürisep, Pinkey Nainwani, Mariam Nakhlé, Juan Ignacio Navarro Horñiacek, Anna Nedoluzhko, Gunta Nešpore-Bērzkalne, Manuela Nevaci, Lương Nguyễn Thị, Huyền Nguyễn Thị Minh, Yoshihiro Nikaido, Vitaly Nikolaev, Rattima Nitisaroj, Alireza Nourian, Hanna Nurmi, Stina Ojala, Atul Kr. Ojha, Adédayọ̀ Olúòkun, Mai Omura, Emeka Onwuegbuzia, Petya Osenova, Robert Östling, Lilja Øvrelid, Şaziye Betül Özateş, Merve Özçelik, Arzucan Özgür, Balkız Öztürk Başaran, Hyunji Hayley Park, Niko Partanen, Elena Pascual, Marco Passarotti, Agnieszka Patejuk, Guilherme Paulino-Passos, Angelika Peljak-Łapińska, Siyao Peng, Cenel-Augusto Perez, Natalia Perkova, Guy Perrier, Slav Petrov, Daria Petrova, Jason Phelan, Jussi Piitulainen, Tommi A Pirinen, Emily Pitler, Barbara Plank, Thierry Poibeau, Larisa Ponomareva, Martin Popel, Lauma Pretkalniņa, Sophie Prévost, Prokopis Prokopidis, Adam Przepiórkowski, Tiina Puolakainen, Sampo Pyysalo, Peng Qi, Andriela Rääbis, Alexandre Rademaker, Taraka Rama, Loganathan Ramasamy, Carlos Ramisch, Fam Rashel, Mohammad Sadegh Rasooli, Vinit Ravishankar, Livy Real, Petru Rebeja, Siva Reddy, Georg Rehm, Ivan Riabov, Michael Rießler, Erika Rimkutė, Larissa Rinaldi, Laura Rituma, Luisa Rocha, Eiríkur Rögnvaldsson, Mykhailo Romanenko, Rudolf Rosa, Valentin Roșca, Davide Rovati, Olga Rudina, Jack Rueter, Kristján Rúnarsson, Shoval Sadde, Pegah Safari, Benoît Sagot, Aleksi Sahala, Shadi Saleh, Alessio Salomoni, Tanja Samardžić, Stephanie Samson, Manuela Sanguinetti, Ezgi Sanıyar, Dage Särg, Baiba Saulīte, Yanin Sawanakunanon, Shefali Saxena, Kevin Scannell, Salvatore Scarlata, Nathan Schneider, Sebastian Schuster, Lane Schwartz, Djamé Seddah, Wolfgang Seeker, Mojgan Seraji, Mo Shen, Atsuko Shimada, Hiroyuki Shirasu, Yana Shishkina, Muh Shohibussirri, Dmitry Sichinava, Janine Siewert, Einar Freyr Sigurðsson, Aline Silveira, Natalia Silveira, Maria Simi, Radu Simionescu, Katalin Simkó, Mária Šimková, Kiril Simov, Maria Skachedubova, Aaron Smith, Isabela Soares-Bastos, Carolyn Spadine, Rachele Sprugnoli, Steinhór Steingrímsson, Antonio Stella, Milan Straka, Emmett Strickland, Jana Strnadová, Alane Suhr, Yogi Lesmana Sulestio, Umut Sulubacak, Shingo Suzuki, Zsolt Szántó, Dima Taji, Yuta Takahashi, Fabio Tamburini, Mary Ann C. Tan, Takaaki Tanaka, Samson Tella, Isabelle Tellier, Marinella Testori, Guillaume Thomas, Liisi Torga, Marsida Toska, Trond Trosterud, Anna Trukhina, Reut Tsarfaty, Utku Türk, Francis Tyers, Sumire Uematsu, Roman Untilov, Zdeňka Urešová, Larraitz Uria, Hans Uszkoreit, Andrius Utka, Sowmya Vajjala, Rob van der Goot, Martine Vanhove, Daniel van Niekerk, Gertjan van Noord, Viktor Varga, Eric Villemonte de la Clergerie, Veronika Vincze, Natalia Vlasova, Aya Wakasa,

Joel C. Wallenberg, Lars Wallin, Abigail Walsh, Jing Xian Wang, Jonathan North Washington, Maximilan Wendt, Paul Widmer, Seyi Williams, Mats Wirén, Christian Wittern, Tsegay Woldemariam, Tak-sum Wong, Alina Wróblewska, Mary Yako, Kayo Yamashita, Naoki Yamazaki, Chunxiao Yan, Koichi Yasuoka, Marat M. Yavrumyan, Arife Betül Yenice, Olcay Taner Yıldız, Zhuoran Yu, Zdeněk Žabokrtský, Shorouq Zahra, Amir Zeldes, Hanzhi Zhu, Anna Zhuravleva, and Rayan Ziane. 2021. Universal dependencies 2.8.1. LINDAT/CLARIAH-CZ digital library at the Institute of Formal and Applied Linguistics (ÚFAL), Faculty of Mathematics and Physics, Charles University.

A Clause Representations

The three clauses from Figure 1 are represented as follows (using GFs for composite verbs):

$$\begin{bmatrix} \text{CLAUSE\_DEPREL} & \text{discourse} \\ \text{CLAUSE\_POS} & \text{INTJ} \\ \text{DISC\_DISCOURSE\_DEPREL} & \text{discourse} \\ \text{DISC\_DISCOURSE\_POS} & \text{INTJ} \end{bmatrix} \quad (7)$$

$$\begin{bmatrix} \text{CLAUSE\_DEPREL} & \text{root} \\ \text{CLAUSE\_POS} & \text{VERB} \\ \text{CLAUSE\_PREC} & , \\ \text{CLAUSE\_SUCC} & . \\ \text{NP\_NSUBJ\_CASE} & \text{Nom} \\ \text{NP\_NSUBJ\_DEPREL} & \text{nsubj} \\ \text{NP\_NSUBJ\_NUMBER} & \text{Sing} \\ \text{NP\_NSUBJ\_PERSON} & 1 \\ \text{NP\_NSUBJ\_POS} & \text{PRON} \\ \text{NP\_NSUBJ\_PRONTYPE} & \text{Prs} \\ \text{VERB\_ASPECT} & \text{Imp} \\ \text{VERB\_MOOD} & \text{Ind} \\ \text{VERB\_TENSE} & \text{Fut} \\ \text{VERB\_VERBFORM} & \text{Fin} \\ \text{VERB\_VOICE} & \text{Act} \end{bmatrix} \quad (8)$$

$$\begin{bmatrix} \text{CLAUSE\_DEPREL} & \text{xcomp} \\ \text{CLAUSE\_POS} & \text{VERB} \\ \text{NP\_OBJ\_DEFINITE} & \text{Ind} \\ \text{NP\_OBJ\_DEPREL} & \text{obj} \\ \text{NP\_OBJ\_NUMBER} & \text{Sing} \\ \text{NP\_OBJ\_POS} & \text{NOUN} \\ \text{NP\_OBJ\_PRONTYPE} & \text{Art} \\ \text{VERB\_VERBFORM} & \text{Inf} \end{bmatrix} \quad (9)$$

The prefix `clause`, `NP`, `verb` or `disc` corresponds to the syntactic unit as described in Sections 3.1–3.4.

B Decision Tree

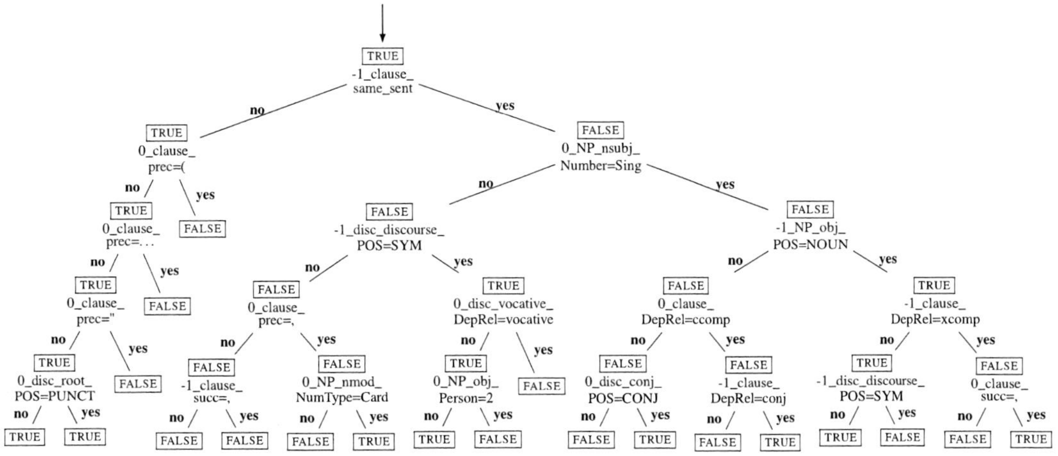

Figure 3: Decision tree learned on `eng.sdrt.stac` (using GFSs). "TRUE" are segment starts. The number prefixed to a feature is the offset to the current clause, e.g. feature of the preceding clause start with "-1".

A Unified Approach to Discourse Relation Classification in nine Languages

Hanna Varachkina
University of Göttingen, Germany
Department of German Philology
hanna.varachkina@
stud.uni-goettingen.de

Franziska Pannach
University of Göttingen, Germany
Göttingen Centre for Digital Humanities
franziska.pannach@
uni-goettingen.de

Abstract

This paper presents efforts to solve the shared task on discourse relation classification (disrpt task 3). The intricate prediction task aims to predict a large number of classes from the Rhetorical Structure Theory (RST) framework for nine target languages. Labels include discourse relations such as *background*, *condition*, *contrast* and *elaboration*. We present an approach using euclidean distance between sentence embeddings that were extracted using multlingual sentence BERT (sBERT) and directionality as features. The data was combined into five classes which were used for initial prediction. The second classification step predicts the target classes. We observe a substantial difference in results depending on the number of occurrences of the target label in the training data. We achieve the best results on Chinese, where our system achieves 70 % accuracy on 20 labels.

1 Introduction

Discourse relations are an integral part of natural language understanding. They provide information on the interaction between aspects of utterances, such as *result* "I had already seen the movie, so the ending of the book was spoiled!" or *contrast* "I did not like her first book, but her latest novel is great!". In natural language processing, understanding discourse relations is beneficial for many tasks, e.g. the classification of sentiment (Benamara et al., 2016).

Due to different frameworks and the complexity of the subject, the classification of discourse relations is a challenging task that has been addressed by the Shared Task on Discourse Relation Classification across Formalisms (Task 3 of the workshop on Discourse Relation Parsing and Treebanking (DISRPT))[1]. The proposed shared task is to our knowledge the first of its kind on discourse relation classification across formalisms.

In the past, a number of classification efforts for the data created within the PDTB framework and RST (Hernault et al., 2010; Liu et al., 2016; Kim et al., 2020), mostly for English have been attempted. This paper focuses on the data based on the Rhetorical Structure Theory (RST) of nine languages: Basque, Chinese, Dutch, English, Farsi, German, Portuguese, Russian and Spanish in a cross-lingual approach.

2 Data

The data sets created on the basis of RST were used for the task of discourse relation classification, since the text data for most other data sets was hidden by underscores and we did not have resources to restore it. Out of two data sets provided for Spanish the RST Spanish Treebank (spa.rst.rststb) was chosen. Due to the lack of the original text data, the rows with units hidden by underscores were removed from the English data set (Georgetown University Multilayer corpus – eng.rst.gum). This reduced English model was trained for comparison with other models.

The RST corpora were analyzed and compared. We found that they have different size, e.g. the Chinese data set is the smallest and the Russian data set exceeds the size of all the other data sets.

The corpora for different languages differ in their number of labels. Only the labels *background*, *condition*, *contrast* and *elaboration* appear in all languages. Table 1 shows the distribution of labels between languages based on their training, development and test sets combined. The second to last column shows unique labels, 57 in total for all languages. Some labels of different languages differ slightly in spelling. Those were considered as one (e.g. *antithesis* and *anthitesis*). In Span-

[1]https://sites.google.com/georgetown.edu/disrpt2021

Proceedings of the 2nd Shared Task on Discourse Relation Parsing and Treebanking (DISRPT 2021), pages 46–50
November 11, 2021. ©2021 Association for Computational Linguistics

German	English	Basque	Farsi	Dutch	Portuguese	Russian	Spanish	Chinese	Unique labels	Class
							alternative		alternative	0
antithesis	antithesis	antithesis		antithesis	antithesis	antithesis	antithesis	antithesis	antithesis	0
	attribution		attribution		attribution	attribution		attribution	attribution	4
background	background	background	background	background	background	background	backgroun(d)	background	background	4
cause	cause	cause	cause			cause	cause	cause	cause	2
						cause-effect			cause-effect	2
circumstance	circumstance	circumstance		circumstance	circumstance		circumstance	circumstance	circumstance	4
			comparison		comparison	comparison			comparison	0
concession	concession	concession		concession	concession	concession	concession	concession	concession	0
					conclusion	conclusion			conclusion	2
condition	condition	condition	condition	condition	condition	condition	condition	condition	condition	0
conjunction		conjunction		conjunction			conjunction	conjunction	conjunction	3
contrast	contrast	contrast	contrast	contrast	contrast	contrast	contrast	contrast	contrast	0
disjunction		disjunction		disjunction			disjunction	disjunction	disjunction	3
						effect			effect	2
e-elaboration									e-elaboration	4
elaboration	elaboration	elaboration	elaboration	elaboration	elaboration	elaboration	elaboration	elaboration	elaboration	4
		enablement	enablement	enablement	enablement		enablement	enablement	enablement	4
	evaluation	evaluation	evaluation	evaluation	evaluation	evaluation	evaluation	evaluation	evaluation	1
evaluation-n									evaluation-n	1
evaluation-s									evaluation-s	1
evidence	evidence	evidence		evidence	evidence	evidence	evidence	evidence	evidence	4
			explanation		explanation				explanation	4
interpretation		interpretation		interpretation	interpretation		interpretation	interpretation	interpretation	1
						interpretation-evaluation			interpretation-evaluation	1
joint	joint	joint	joint	joint	joint	joint	joint		joint	3
	justify	justify		justify	justify		justify	justify	justify	1
list		list		list	list		list	list	list	3
	manner								manner	2
			manner-means						manner-means	2
means	means	means		means	means		means	means	means	2
	motivation	motibation		motivation	motivation	motivation	motivation	motivation	motivation	2
				nonvolitional-cause	non-volitional-cause				non-volitional-cause	2
					non-volitional-cause-e				non-volitional-cause-e	2
				nonvolitional-result	non-volitional-result				non-volitional-result	2
					non-volitional-result-e				non-volitional-result-e	2
		otherwise		otherwise	otherwise				otherwise	0
					parenthetical				parenthetical	4
preparation	preparation	preparation		preparation		preparation	preparation	preparation	preparation	4
purpose	purpose	purpose		purpose	purpose	purpose	purpose	purpose	purpose	2
	question								question	4
reason									reason	2
restatement	restatement	restatement		restatement	restatement	restatement	restatement	restatement	restatement	4
				restatement-mn					restatement-mn	4
result	result	result					result	result	result	2
sequence	sequence	sequence		sequence	sequence	sequence	sequence	sequence	sequence	3
solutionhood	solutionhood	solution-hood		solutionhood	solutionhood	solutionhood	solutionhood	solutionhood	solutionhood	4
				span					span	3
summary		summary	summary	summary			summary	summary	summary	4
			temporal						temporal	3
			topichange						topichange	4
			topicomment						topicomment	4
			topidrift						topidrift	4
		unconditional		unconditional					unconditional	0
		unless		unless			unless		unless	0
				volitional-cause	volitional-cause				volitional-cause	2
				volitional-result	volitional-result				volitional-result	2

Table 1: All labels and their assignment to five large categories: 0, 1, 2, 3, 4.

ish, *backgroun* in the train and *background* in the development sets were considered as one label.

In all cases except English (after removing rows with underscores), the number of labels in the test set is smaller than in the train and development sets combined (see Table 2). For Portuguese, this difference is the largest with the test set containing 11 labels less than the training set. In case of Dutch, the test data contains one instance with the label *span* that is not present neither in the train nor in the development set. Apart from that, all labels in the test sets of the other languages occur in their train and/or the development sets and can be learnt.

The number of labels in each data set is large (between 16 and 29), so that it is quite difficult for any classifier to distinguish between them. Inspired by other discourse relation schemes such as PDTB (Prasad et al., 2008) that suggests hierarchical labels, unique labels were mapped to five large classes (last column in Table 1) as some of them can be seen as subclasses of the other. This was done in order to break down the task of classifying a very large number of classes as will be described in the next section. Figure 1 shows which classes are grouped together.

3 Method

The subject of discourse relation classification are not text units, but rather relations between them. One of the methods for comparing two text units is to calculate euclidean distance between their embeddings. Using multilingual sBERT (Reimers and Gurevych, 2020) models, embeddings for two discourse units were obtained [2]. The first version of the model created for 15 languages (Yang et al., 2020) was used for the corresponding languages in the shared task data set. Its second version for a larger number of languages was used for the re-

[2] https://www.sbert.net/docs/pretrained_models.html

Class 0 Contrast	Class 1 Evaluation	Class 2 Reason	Class 3 Set	Class 4 Context
Alternative	Evaluation	Cause	Conjunction	Attribution
Antithesis	Evaluation-m	Cause-effect	Disjunction	Background
Comparison	Evaluation-s	Conclusion	Joint	E-Elaboration
Concession	Interpretation	Effect	List	Elaboration
Condition	Interpretation-Evaluation	Manner	Sequence	Enablement
Contrast	Justify	Manner-means	Span	Evidence
Otherwise		Means	Temporal	Explanation
Unconditional		Non-volitional-cause		Parenthetical
Unless		Non-volitional-cause-e		Preparation
		Non-volitional-result		Restatement
		Non-volitional-cause-e		Restatement-mn
		Purpose		Solutionhood
		Reason		Summary
		Result		Topichange
		Volitional-cause		Topicomment
		Volitional-result		Topidrift

Figure 1: Five classes used for first level training

maining languages in the data sets, since the second model works slightly worse on the languages from the first model. Then euclidean distance between the embeddings of these two units was calculated. The euclidean distance is the first feature for the model and the second is a categorical one taken from the column that indicate the directionality information. Initially, we experimented with several embeddings for the German corpus, but the results were similar, including those for the multilingual embeddings. Therefore, we used the same multilingual model for several languages for simplicity reasons.

Using the features mentioned above, a stacked random forest model was trained with one-versus-all approach and balanced weights for classes. The model parameters were the same for all the layers of the stacked model. Since the number of original classes is very large, the labels were grouped into larger classes as the last column in Table 1 shows. The original training and development sets were combined and split, so that the development set comprises 40 % of the combined one. This development set was used for testing a random forest model for five upper classes. After training the model, the predictions for large classes were mapped to the original labels. Now the test set of the classifier for large classes (the development set after resizing) was used for training five models, one for each large class that classify the original labels contained in the large class. The predictions of five models were compared with the original test data for evaluation. As for the Chinese data set, the original training set was duplicated into the development set in order to avoid spareness, while all the other steps in the model were the same as described above.

4 Results

Poorly predicted large classes set restrictions on further label classification. Some of the classes have very few instances so that models cannot learn and recognize them properly. Table 4 shows F1-score results for individual labels in the Chinese data set. Out of 20 original classes in the test data, 10 were not recognized correctly, i.e. exactly a half, which is one of the highest numbers of neglected classes among languages. This can be explained by the fact that the number of train instances for these classes is extremely low. Russian (Table 5) is the language with the smallest number of labels that were not recognized (only 2). It is also the largest data set with a sufficient number of instances for most labels to train and test a model on.

In general, the smaller the number of classes and the larger the data set (and the number of instances for each label), the better is the accuracy score. As can be seen in Table 2, the results range from 35 % accuracy for German to 70 % for Chinese. Although half of the labels for Chinese were not recognized, the remaining labels were recognized very well, which led to a high overall accuracy. For example, the *elaboration* label has 69 instances in the test set and receives 93 % F1-score, while the *evidence* label has only one instance and receives 0 % F1-score, see Table 4.

Language	Test set length	Unique labels	Test labels	Acc.
German	260	26	24	0.35
English	1800	23	23	0.49
Basque	667	29	26	0.44
Farsi	592	17	16	0.59
Dutch	324	33	29	0.45
Portuguese	263	32	21	0.49
Russian	2838	22	20	0.61
Spanish	426	28	25	0.45
Chinese	159	26	20	0.70

Table 2: Evaluation results on RST data sets. The English data is taken after removing underscores.

The organizers of the shared task evaluated our model on all data sets, including non-RST data that we did not have access to due to accessibility restrictions. Additional labels from the non-RST data sets should be regarded separately from the labels in Table 1. Since we did not have text data, we decided not to judge whether they fit into the thematic categories in Figure 1. The organizers assigned these additional labels successively to each category (so the first additional relation gets group 1, the next gets group 2, and so on in a rotation). The results can be observed in Table 3. The data sets with anonymized data were included into evaluation and the English data GUM that was partially anonymized was included entirely. Beside the sparse Chinese data set (zho.rst.sctb), the Spanish version of the same corpus (spa.rst.sctb) as well as the French data set (fra.sdrt.annodis) are also sparse. Therefore, the training set was duplicated into the development set. As for the results, the accuracy for the English data set including the hidden text units drops from 49 % to 47 %. As for the Spanish data sets, the score for the corpus that we chose (spa.rst.rststb) is lower than for the second Spanish corpus (spa.rst.sctb), 45 % compared to 69 %. On average, we reach 54 % accuracy.

Test set	Acc.
deu.rst.pcc	0.35
eng.pdtb.pdtb	0.50
eng.rst.gum	0.47
eng.rst.rstdt	0.55
eng.sdrt.stac	0.54
eus.rst.ert	0.44
fas.rst.prstc	0.59
fra.sdrt.annodis	0.46
nld.rst.nldt	0.45
por.rst.cstn	0.49
rus.rst.rrt	0.61
spa.rst.rststb	0.45
spa.rst.sctb	0.69
tur.pdtb.tdb	0.48
zho.pdtb.cdtb	0.89
zho.rst.sctb	0.70
Average	0.54

Table 3: Evaluation results from the organizers. The RST data sets from Table 2 are in bold.

5 Conclusion

Although the data taken for this shared task is based on the Rhetorical Structure Theory, each language (and corpus) proposes a different set of labels for classification. However, in many cases there are substantial overlaps which makes a unified approach to discourse relation classification possible.

This paper suggests such an approach by grouping all unique labels, some of which are shared between languages, to large classes and using a stacked random forest model in each case. However, a different division into larger groups, for example using automatic approaches such as clustering could be beneficial and reduce the amount of manual work. Further fine-tuning of the embeddings with the shared task data will potentially improve the results. As for the random forest method, different hyperparameters for different languages can be tried out in additional experiments.

We show that our approach achieves good results on labels with a sufficient amount of instances per class across languages. Albeit the simplicity of the model and small number features, we achieve 70 % accuracy on Chinese labels and at least 35 % for German.

Label (test)	F1-score (test)	Support (test)	Support (dev set)
antithesis	0.40	3	5
background	0.00	4	13
circumstance	0.00	4	4
condition	1.00	1	6
conjunction	0.00	2	3
contrast	0.33	5	2
disjunction	0.00	2	4
elaboration	0.93	69	114
enablement	0.00	1	1
evidence	0.00	1	3
interpretation	0.50	3	5
list	0.84	32	80
means	0.00	2	7
motivation	0.00	1	2
preparation	0.73	12	48
purpose	0.36	6	11
restatement	0.00	1	0
result	0.25	4	8
sequence	0.22	5	12
summary	0.00	1	5
additional label in dev set			
cause	0.00	0	6
justify	0.00	0	3
concession	0.00	0	8
solutionhood	0.00	0	1
		159	351

Table 4: Classification results for Chinese

Label (test)	F1-score (test)	Support (test)	Support (dev set)
antithesis	0.00	2	12
attribution	0.18	58	688
background	0.12	68	299
cause	0.58	208	930
cause-effect	0.04	27	123
comparison	0.08	41	236
concession	0.06	27	156
condition	0.59	173	635
contrast	0.61	202	850
effect	0.00	1	27
elaboration	0.82	701	2899
evaluation	0.86	135	520
evidence	0.04	73	329
interpretation -evaluation	0.14	15	65
joint	0.83	671	3017
preparation	0.49	149	671
purpose	0.31	92	506
restatement	0.08	24	114
sequence	0.16	150	455
solutionhood	0.08	26	156
additional label in dev set			
conclusion	0.00	0	2
		2843	12690

Table 5: Classification results for Russian

References

Farah Benamara, Maite Taboada, and Yannick Mathieu. 2016. Evaluative language beyond bags of words: Linguistic insights and computational applications. *Computational Linguistics*, 43:1–103.

Hugo Hernault, Danushka Bollegala, and Mitsuru Ishizuka. 2010. Towards semi-supervised classification of discourse relations using feature correlations. In *Proceedings of the SIGDIAL 2010 Conference*, pages 55–58.

Najoung Kim, Song Feng, Chulaka Gunasekara, and Luis Lastras. 2020. Implicit discourse relation classification: We need to talk about evaluation. In *Proceedings of the 58th Annual Meeting of the Association for Computational Linguistics*, pages 5404–5414, Online. Association for Computational Linguistics.

Yang Liu, Sujian Li, Xiaodong Zhang, and Zhifang Sui. 2016. Implicit discourse relation classification via multi-task neural networks. In *Proceedings of the AAAI Conference on Artificial Intelligence*, volume 30.

Rashmi Prasad, Nikhil Dinesh, Alan Lee, Eleni Miltsakaki, Livio Robaldo, Aravind K Joshi, and Bonnie L Webber. 2008. The penn discourse treebank 2.0. In *Proceedings of the 6th Language Resources and Evaluation Conference*.

Nils Reimers and Iryna Gurevych. 2020. Making monolingual sentence embeddings multilingual using knowledge distillation. In *Proceedings of the 2020 Conference on Empirical Methods in Natural Language Processing*.

Yinfei Yang, Daniel Cer, Amin Ahmad, Mandy Guo, Jax Law, Noah Constant, Gustavo Hernandez Abrego, Steve Yuan, Chris Tar, Yun-hsuan Sung, Brian Strope, and Ray Kurzweil. 2020. Multilingual universal sentence encoder for semantic retrieval. In *Proceedings of the 58th Annual Meeting of the Association for Computational Linguistics: System Demonstrations*, pages 87–94, Online. Association for Computational Linguistics.

DisCoDisCo at the DISRPT2021 Shared Task: A System for Discourse Segmentation, Classification, and Connective Detection

Luke Gessler, Shabnam Behzad, Yang Janet Liu, Siyao Peng, Yilun Zhu, Amir Zeldes
Corpling Lab
Georgetown University
{lg876, sb1796, yl879, sp1184, yz565, az364}@georgetown.edu

Abstract

This paper describes our submission to the DISRPT2021 Shared Task on Discourse Unit Segmentation, Connective Detection, and Relation Classification. Our system, called DisCoDisCo, is a Transformer-based neural classifier which enhances contextualized word embeddings (CWEs) with hand-crafted features, relying on tokenwise sequence tagging for discourse segmentation and connective detection, and a feature-rich, encoder-less sentence pair classifier for relation classification. Our results for the first two tasks outperform SOTA scores from the previous 2019 shared task, and results on relation classification suggest strong performance on the new 2021 benchmark. Ablation tests show that including features beyond CWEs are helpful for both tasks, and a partial evaluation of multiple pre-trained Transformer-based language models indicates that models pre-trained on the Next Sentence Prediction (NSP) task are optimal for relation classification.*

1 Introduction

Recent years have seen tremendous advances in NLP systems' ability to handle discourse level phenomena, including discourse unit segmentation and connective detection (Zeldes et al., 2019) as well as discourse relation classification (e.g. Lin et al. 2014; Braud et al. 2017a; Kobayashi et al. 2021). For segmentation and connective detection, the current state of the art (SOTA) is provided by models using Transformer-based, pretrained contextualized word embeddings (Muller et al., 2019), focusing on large context windows without implementation of hand-crafted features. For relation classification, SOTA performance on the English RST-DT benchmark (Carlson et al., 2003) has been achieved by neural approaches (Guz and Carenini, 2020; Kobayashi et al., 2020; Nguyen et al., 2021; Kobayashi et al., 2021). For PDTB-style data, the 2015 and 2016 CoNLL shared tasks on shallow discourse parsing (Xue et al., 2015, 2016) have motivated work on both explicit (e.g. Kido and Aizawa 2016) and implicit (e.g. Liu et al. 2016; Wang and Lan 2016; Rutherford et al. 2017; Kim et al. 2020; Liang et al. 2020; Zhang et al. 2021) discourse relation classification in English PDTB-2 (Prasad et al., 2008) and PDTB-3 (Prasad et al., 2019) as well as on the PDTB-style Chinese newswire corpus (CDTB, Zhou and Xue 2012; Zhou et al. 2014) such as Schenk et al. (2016) and Weiss and Bajec (2016).

Our system for DISRPT 2021, called DisCoDisCo, (**Dis**trict of **Co**lumbia **Dis**course **Co**gnoscente) extends the current SOTA architecture by introducing hand-crafted categorical and numerical features that represent salient aspects of documents' structural and linguistic properties. While Transformer-based contextualized word embeddings (CWEs) have proven to be rich in linguistic features, they are not perfect (Rogers et al., 2020), and there are some textual features—such as position of a sentence within a document, or the number of identical words occurring in two discourse units—which are difficult or impossible for a typical Transformer-based CWE model to know. We therefore supplement CWEs with hand-crafted features in our model, with special attention paid to features we expect CWEs to have a poor grasp of.

We implement our system with a pretrained Transformer-based contextualized word embedding model at its core, and dense embeddings of our hand-crafted features incorporated into it. Our exact approach varies by task: we use a tokenwise classification approach for EDU segmentation, a CRF-based sequence tagger for connective detection, and a BERT pooling classifier for relation classification. Our system is implemented in Py-

*Full disclosure: our team includes both organizers and dataset annotators from the shared task. All code is available at `https://github.com/gucorpling/DisCoDisCo`

Proceedings of the 2nd Shared Task on Discourse Relation Parsing and Treebanking (DISRPT 2021), pages 51–62
November 11, 2021.

Torch (Paszke et al., 2019) using the framework AllenNLP (Gardner et al., 2018). Our results show SOTA scores exceeding comparable numbers from the 2019 shared task, and ablation studies indicate the contribution of features beyond CWEs.

2 Previous Work

Segmentation and Connective Detection Following the era of rule-based segmenters (e.g. Marcu 2000, Thanh et al. 2004), Soricut and Marcu (2003) used probabilistic models over constituent trees for token-wise binary classification (i.e. boundary/no-boundary). Sporleder and Lapata (2005) used a two-level stacked boosting classifier on chunks, POS tags, tokens and sentence lengths, among other features. Hernault et al. (2010) used an SVM over token and POS trigrams as well as phrase structure trees.

More recently, Braud et al. (2017b) used bi-LSTM-CRF sequence labeling on dependency parses, with words, POS tags, dependency relations, parent, grandparent, and dependency direction, achieving an F_1 of 89.5 on the English RST-DT benchmark (Carlson et al., 2003) with parser-predicted syntax. Approaches using CWEs as the only input feature (Muller et al., 2019) have achieved an F_1 of 96.04 on the same dataset with gold sentence splits and 93.43 without, while for some smaller English and non-English datasets, approaches incorporating features and word embeddings remain superior (e.g. for English STAC and GUM, as well as Dutch RST data, Yu et al. 2019; and for Chinese, Bourgonje and Schäfer 2019; for more on these datasets see below).

For connective detection, Pitler and Nenkova (2009) used a MaxEnt classifier with syntactic features extracted from gold Penn Treebank (Marcus et al., 1993) parses of PDTB (Prasad et al., 2008) articles. Patterson and Kehler (2013) presented a logistic regression model trained on eight relation types from PDTB, with features in three categories: *Relation-level* such as the connective signaling the relation; *Argument-level* such as size or complexity of argument spans; and *Discourse-level* features, targeting dependencies between the relation and its neighboring relations in the text (cf. our approach to featurizing overall utilization of argument spans in the data below). Polepalli Ramesh et al. (2012) used SVM and CRF to identify connectives in biomedical texts (Prasad et al., 2011), with features such as POS tags, dependencies and domain-specific semantic features included several biomedical gene/species taggers, in addition to predicted biomedical NER features.

Current SOTA approaches rely on sequence labeling in a BIO scheme with CWEs from either plain text (Muller et al., 2019) or integrating word embeddings and dependency tree features (POS, dependencies, phrase spans, Yu et al. 2019), dependending on the dataset and availability of gold standard features.

Discourse Relation Classification Generally speaking, discourse relation classification assigns a relation label to two pieces of texts from a set of predefined coherence or rhetorical relation labels (Stede, 2011), which varies across different discourse frameworks, corpora, and languages. Given different perspectives and theoretical frameworks, the implementation and evaluation of the relation classification task varies considerably.

In Rhetorical Structure Theory (RST, Mann and Thompson 1988), discourse relations hold between spans of text and are hierarchically represented in a tree structure (Zeldes, 2018). Performance is evaluated and reported using the micro-averaged, standard Parseval scores for a binary tree representation, following Morey et al. (2017). Current SOTA performance (Kobayashi et al., 2021) on the English RST-DT benchmark (Carlson et al., 2003) with gold segmentation achieved a micro-averaged original Parseval score of 54.1 by utilizing both a span-based neural parser (Kobayashi et al., 2020) and a two-staged transition-based SVM parser (Wang et al., 2017) as well as leveraging silver data.

Since PDTB is a lexically grounded framework, discourse relation classification is also called sense classification in PDTB-style discourse parsing: a sense label is assigned to the discourse connective between two text spans when a discourse connective is present (i.e. explicit relation classification) or a label is assigned to an adjacent pair of sentences when no discourse connective is present (i.e. implicit relation classification) (Jurafsky and Martin, 2020). Explicit relation classification is easier as the presence of the connective itself is considered the best signal of the relation label. Most systems from the 2016 CoNLL shared task on shallow discourse parsing adopted machine learning techniques such as SVM and MaxEnt with hand-crafted features (Xue et al., 2016). For instance, for the English PDTB-2 (Prasad et al., 2008), Kido and Aizawa (2016) achieved the best performance (an F_1 = 90.22) on the explicit relation classification task by implementing a majority classifier and a MaxEnt classifier while Wang and Lan (2016) achieved the best performance (F_1 = 40.91) on implicit relation classification using a convolutional neural network. Wang and Lan (2016) also achieved the best performance on the Chinese CDTB dataset (Zhou and Xue, 2012) in the implicit relation classification task.

More recent work on implicit relation classification has adopted a graph-based context tracking network to model the necessary context for interpreting the discourse and has gained better performance on PDTB-2 (Zhang et al., 2021). In addition, the increase in the number of implicit relation instances in PDTB-3 (Prasad et al., 2019) has sparked more interest in exploring their recognition, such as Kim et al. (2020) and Liang et al. (2020). Kim et al. (2020) presented the first set of results on implicit relation classification for both top-level senses (four labels) and more fined-grained level-2 senses (amounting to 11 labels) in PDTB-3 from two strong sentence encoder models using BERT (Devlin et al., 2019) and XLNet (Yang et al., 2019). Due to the novelty of the DISRPT 2021 relation classification task, which combines implicit and explicit relation classification across frameworks for an unlabeled graph structure, comparable scores do not yet exist at the time of writing.

3 Approach

Our system comprises two main components: one targeting segmentation and connective detection using neural sequence tagging (as binary classification and BIO tagging respectively), and one targeting relation classification using BERT (Devlin et al., 2019) fine-tuning. We further enhance both components with the use of hand-crafted categorical and numeric features by encoding them in dense embeddings and introducing them into our neural models.

3.1 Segmentation and Connective Detection

Our model for segmentation and connective detection is structured as a sequence tagging model, as might be used for a task like POS tagging or entity recognition: the text is embedded, encoded with a single bi-LSTM, and decoded.

In the embedding layer, we rely on three kinds of embeddings: bi-LSTM encoded character embeddings (d = 64); language-specific fastText (Bojanowski et al., 2017) static word embeddings (d = 300); and language-specific contextualized word embeddings from pretrained models posted publicly on HuggingFace's model registry at `huggingface.co` and used via HuggingFace's `transformers` library (Wolf et al., 2020) (d = 768/1024). The fastText embeddings are kept frozen during training, but the pretrained Transformer model's parameters are trainable, at a lower learning rate. Average pooling is used to obtain word-level representations from CWE sub-word representations. Multiple CWEs were evaluated for each language, and the one that yielded the best performance on the validation splits of the corpora for that language was selected, shown in Table 1. These three representations are concatenated, yielding a vector of size d_{emb} for each word.

In the next layer, we encode the embeddings along with a variety of features and a representation of the preceding and following sentence (see below). The features we compute are tokenwise, and cover a variety of grammatical and textual information that we expected would be useful for the task. Some of the features are described in Table 2. In order to convert these features into tensors, every categorical feature is embedded in a space as big as the square root of the total number of labels for the feature, and every numerical feature is log scaled. This yields an additional d_{feat} dimensions for each word.

In addition to the features, we also compute a representation of the current sentence's two neighboring sentences by embedding them and using a bi-LSTM to summarize them into a relatively low-dimensional ($d_{\text{neighbors}}$ = 400) vector, which is concatenated onto every word's vector. Combining the feature dimensions and the neighboring sentences' dimensions, our input to the encoder is of size $d_{\text{enc}} = d_{\text{emb}} + d_{\text{feat}} + d_{\text{neighbors}}$.

The sequence is fed through a bi-LSTM, and the label for each token is then predicted either by a linear projection layer or conditional random fields: CRF is used for connective detection datasets, and the linear projection layer is used for segmentation datasets.[b]

For the plain text segmentation scenario, we generate automatic sentence splits and Universal Dependencies parses using the Transformer-based sentence splitter used in the AMALGUM

[b]We initially used a CRF on all datasets, but our experiments showed a small degradation on segmentation datasets when using CRF.

Lng.	Segmentation/Connective Detection	Relation Classification
deu	xlm-roberta-large	bert-base-german-cased
eng	google/electra-large-discriminator	bert-base-cased
eus	ixa-ehu/berteus-base-cased	ixa-ehu/berteus-base-cased
fas	HooshvareLab/bert-fa-base-uncased	HooshvareLab/bert-fa-base-uncased
fra	xlm-roberta-large	dbmdz/bert-base-french-europeana-cased
nld	pdelobelle/robbert-v2-dutch-base	GroNLP/bert-base-dutch-cased
por	neuralmind/bert-base-portuguese-cased	neuralmind/bert-base-portuguese-cased
rus	DeepPavlov/rubert-base-cased	DeepPavlov/rubert-base-cased-sentence
spa	dccuchile/bert-base-spanish-wwm-cased	dccuchile/bert-base-spanish-wwm-cased
tur	dbmdz/bert-base-turkish-cased	dbmdz/bert-base-turkish-cased
zho	bert-base-chinese	hfl/chinese-bert-wwm-ext

Table 1: CWE Models used, by language. All models were obtained from `huggingface.co`'s registry. Note that there is one exception for relation classification: on `eng.sdrt.stac`, `bert-base-uncased` is used.

Feature	Type	Example	Description
UPOS tag	Cat.	PROPN	UD POS tag
XPOS tag	Cat.	NNP	Language-specific POS tag
UD deprel	Cat.	advmod	UD dependency relation
Head distance	Num.	5	Distance from a word to its head in its UD tree
Sentence type	Cat.	subjunctive	Captures mood and other high-level sentential features
Genre	Cat.	reddit	Genre of a document (where available, as in `eng.rst.gum`)
Sentence length	Num.	23	Length, in tokens, of a sentence.

Table 2: Summary of 7 of the 12 features used for the segmentation and connective detection module. Every categorical feature is embedded in a space whose size is the square root of the total number of labels for the feature, and numerical features are log scaled.

corpus (Gessler et al., 2020) trained on the treebanked shared task training data, tagged using Stanza (Qi et al., 2020) and parsed using DiaParser[c] (Attardi et al., 2021). For `fas.rst.prstc` and `zho.rst.sctb`, we split the text based on punctuation (on '.', '!', '?' and Chinese equivalents) since experiments revealed that this approach yields better sentence boundaries.

3.2 Relation Classification

Our relation classification module has a simple architecture: a pretrained BERT model is used (again varying by language—cf. Table 1), and a linear projection and softmax layer is used on the output of the pooling layer to predict the label of the relation. The two units involved in every relation are prepared just as if they were being prepared for BERT's Next Sentence Prediction (NSP) task: a [CLS] token begins the sequence, a [SEP] token separates the two units in the sequence, and another [SEP] token appears at the end of the sequence. As an example, consider this instance from `eng.sdrt.stac`:

```
[CLS] do we start ?  [SEP] no [SEP]
```

Though this model was originally intended as a baseline, further experiments with e.g. a separate encoder proved to be much less competitive.

Our exact choice of pretrained model differs in most cases from the one used in the segmentation and connective detection task, primarily due to superior performance by models that were pretrained using the NSP task and had a pretrained pooler layer. This restricts the LM choice: for example, most models that are styled after RoBERTa (Liu et al., 2019) are not pretrained using an NSP task. We select models using the same process as before, based on optimal performance on the validation (dev) sets of the corpora.

The system is further enhanced with features. First, the direction feature on each relation is encoded using pseudo-tokens: if the direction of the relation is left to right (1>2), we insert the tokens } and > around the first unit. In the example above, the direction of the relation is left to right (1>2),

[c]https://github.com/Unipisa/diaparser

Feature	Type	Example	Description
Genre	Cat.	reddit	Genre of a document (where available, as in eng.rst.gum)
Children*	Num.	2	No. of child discourse units each unit in the pair has
Discontinuous*	Cat.	false	Whether the unit's tokens are not all contiguous in the text
Is Sentence*	Cat.	true	Whether the unit is a whole sentence
Length Ratio	Num.	0.3	Ratio of unit 1 and unit 2's token lengths
Same Speaker	Cat.	true	Whether the same speaker produced unit 1 and unit 2
Doc. Length	Num.	214	Length of the document, in tokens
Position*	Num.	0.4	Position of the unit in the document, between 0.0 and 1.0
Distance	Num.	7	No. of other discourse units between unit 1 and unit 2
Lexical Overlap	Num.	3	No. of overlapping non-stoplist words in unit 1 and unit 2

Table 3: Sample of features used for the relation classification module. Asterisked features apply twice for each instance, once for each unit. Combination of features varies per corpus—see code for full details.

and the resulting sequence with pseudo-tokens is:

```
[CLS] } do we start ?  > [SEP] no [SEP]
```

The same is done for right-to-left units, where the characters { and < are used instead, but surrounding the second unit:

```
[CLS] thanks [SEP] < im ok { [SEP]
```

Our motivation in doing this is to represent directionality for the BERT encoder in its native feature space, and experimental data show that it is helpful.

Second, we introduce hand-crafted features in a step between the BERT model's embedding and encoder layers. Recall that BERT has a static embedding layer which projects each word-piece into its initial vector representation. Just before this input is sent to the Transformer encoder blocks, we expand the sequence by inserting a new vector in between the [CLS] token and the first token of unit 1. This feature vector bears sequence-level information, where categorical and numerical features have been encoded into a vector just as for the segmentation and connective detection module: numerical features are optionally log scaled or binned and embedded, and categorical features are embedded. The remaining dimensions after all features have been added to the vector are padded with 0.

Unlike our approach for segmentation and connective detection, we change which features we use on a per-corpus basis, as preliminary experiments showed that using all features for all corpora can produce significant degradations, which we hypothesize are caused by feature sparseness in the training split leading to overfitting. A sample of the features we used is in Table 3, and the list of which features were used for which corpus is available in our code.

Specifically, for the LEXICAL OVERLAP feature in the table, we used the freely available stoplists used by the Python library spaCy (Honnibal et al., 2020). The SAME SPEAKER feature has proven very useful in the STAC dataset, which is a corpus of strategic chat conversations (Asher et al., 2016). The DISTANCE feature is used in half of the datasets and has shown effectiveness regardless of annotation framework. Similarly, the POSITION feature has been shown to be beneficial for half of the corpora. The LENGTH RATIO feature proved to be effective for the three PDTB-style datasets. For RST-style corpora, the number of CHILDREN of a nucleus or satellite unit is more effective. Moreover, the DISCONTINUOUS feature has also contributed to performance gain in several RST-style corpora such as `eng.rst.gum`, `eng.rst.rstdt`, `por.rst.cstn`, `spa.rst.rststb`, `zho.rst.sctb`, and `fas.rst.prstc`. The GENRE feature is beneficial in corpora that have a wide range of text types such as `eng.rst.gum`. The direction feature was also included in the feature vector, as experiments showed that including it was helpful, despite the fact that the pseudo-tokens were already expressing it to the BERT encoder.

4 Results

4.1 Segmentation and Connectives

Table 4 gives scores on EDU segmentation and connective detection in the two shared task scenarios: treebanked and plain text, as well as the best previously reported score and system for datasets which are unchanged from 2019 (see Zeldes et al. 2019 for details). We find strong performance in both the

Corpus	P	R	F_1	2019 Best F_1	vs. 2019
deu.rst.pcc	97.07	94.15	**95.58**	94.99 (ToNy)	0.59
eng.rst.gum	93.90	94.43	**94.15**	–	–
eng.rst.rstdt	96.39	96.89	**96.64**	96.04 (ToNy)	0.60
eng.sdrt.stac	96.25	93.63	94.91	**95.32** (GumDrop)	−0.41
eus.rst.ert	93.42	87.73	**90.46**	–	–
fas.rst.prstc	92.79	93.10	**92.94**	–	–
fra.sdrt.annodis	89.43	90.65	**90.02**	–	–
nld.rst.nldt	97.50	94.50	**95.97**	95.45 (GumDrop)	0.52
por.rst.cstn	93.18	95.56	**94.35**	92.92 (ToNy)	1.43
rus.rst.rrt	85.57	86.89	**86.21**	–	–
spa.rst.rststb	92.53	91.96	**92.22**	90.74 (ToNy)	1.48
spa.rst.sctb	83.44	81.55	82.48	**83.12** (ToNy)	−0.64
zho.rst.sctb	90.30	77.38	**83.34**	81.67 (DFKI)	1.67
eng.pdtb.pdtb	92.93	91.15	**92.02**	–	–
tur.pdtb.tdb	93.71	94.53	**94.11**	–	–
zho.pdtb.cdtb	89.19	85.95	**87.52**	–	–
mean	92.35	90.63	91.43	–	–

(a) Results for Gold Treebanked Data.

Corpus	P	R	F_1	2019 Best F_1	vs. 2019	vs. Gold
deu.rst.pcc	95.15	92.86	93.94	**94.68** (ToNy)	−0.74	−1.64
eng.rst.gum	92.65	92.59	**92.61**	–	–	−1.54
eng.rst.rstdt	96.80	95.92	**96.35**	93.43 (ToNy)	2.92	−0.28
eng.sdrt.stac	91.77	92.06	**91.91**	83.99 (ToNy)	7.92	−3.00
eus.rst.ert	92.70	88.38	**90.47**	–	–	0.01
fas.rst.prstc	92.95	92.78	**92.86**	–	–	−0.08
fra.sdrt.annodis	87.95	83.79	**85.78**	–	–	−4.24
nld.rst.nldt	96.97	92.54	**94.69**	92.32 (ToNy)	2.37	−1.29
por.rst.cstn	93.21	95.03	**94.11**	91.86 (ToNy)	2.25	−0.25
rus.rst.rrt	87.31	84.24	**85.74**	–	–	−0.47
spa.rst.rststb	93.30	90.30	**91.76**	89.60 (ToNy)	2.16	−0.46
spa.rst.sctb	83.97	77.98	80.86	**81.65** (ToNy)	−0.79	−1.62
zho.rst.sctb	84.04	70.00	**76.21**	73.10 (GumDrop)	3.08	−7.13
eng.pdtb.pdtb	94.29	90.92	**92.56**	–	–	0.54
tur.pdtb.tdb	91.98	95.22	**93.56**	–	–	−0.55
zho.pdtb.cdtb	90.27	86.54	**88.35**	–	–	0.83
mean	91.58	88.82	90.11	–	–	−1.32

(b) Results for Plain Tokenized Data.

Table 4: Segmentation and Connective Detection Results. All numbers are averaged over five runs in order to accommodate instability in the training process which leads to varying performance. If a corpus was included in the 2019 shared task and has not been significantly modified since then, we also include the best result on the corpus in 2019 for comparison.

treebanked and plain tokenized data scenarios: our system nearly always outperforms the best score from 2019, and we observe especially large gains for connective detection.

On treebanked data, the results show that performance has improved since 2019 on nearly all unchanged datasets, with degradations of only around 0.5% for `eng.sdrt.stac` and `spa.rst.sctb` compared to the previous best systems, GumDrop and ToNy respectively. For some datasets, gains are dramatic, most notably for Turkish (14.5% gain) and Chinese connective detection (8.4%), which is perhaps due to the availability of better language models and our use of conditional random fields. On average the improvement on treebanked data is close to 3% for datasets represented in 2019.

On plain tokenized data, the improvement from 2019 is even more pronounced, with an average gain of 3.7% compared to 2.8% for treebanked data. While performance on some corpora was roughly constant regardless of whether data was treebanked or plain tokenized (e.g. `eng.rst.rstdt`, `por.rst.cstn`), it dropped considerably for some corpora on plain tokenized data. This effect is most dramatic for `zho.rst.sctb`, where we see a degradation of 7.1%. This effect cannot be explained just by the amount of training data available: correlation between training token count and degradation is low (Pearson's $r = 0.092$, $p = 0.74$).

We speculate that these causes of the degradations are primarily due to idiosyncrasies of the corpora. `eng.sdrt.stac`, for instance, has a mild degradation (−3%), which we believe to be primarily due to the lack of punctuation and capitalization compared to e.g. a newswire corpus like `eng.rst.rstdt`, which exhibited very little degradation. From this we might infer that degradation in the absence of treebanked data will be correlated with the degree to which predicting sentence splits from plain text is difficult. We additionally hypothesize that a lack of gold sentence breaks affects RST datasets more than PDTB datasets, since the beginning of a sentence is almost always the beginning of a new elementary discourse unit, while connectives are mainly identified lexically, and need to be identified regardless of the relative position of sentence splits.

Ablation Study In order to assess the importance of the various modules of our segmentation and connective detection system, we conduct an ablation study. Due to the large computational expense of conducting full runs over all datasets, we choose only two ablation conditions. In the first, we remove all handcrafted features described in Table 2. In the second, we remove character embeddings and fastText static word embeddings, leaving only contextualized word embeddings. The results of this study is given in Table 5.

The general trend in the results of the ablation study seems to be that both handcrafted features and supplementary word embeddings are helpful on average, though they may sometimes lead to minor degradations, and have a dramatically pronounced effect on a few corpora in particular. Handcrafted features have a mild effect on most corpora but lead to large gains for GUM, RST-DT, and PDTB. It is not immediately clear why this might be: performance on GUM, which is diverse with respect to genre, probably benefits from having a

Corpus	F_1 (all)	F_1 (no feats.)		F_1 (CWE only)	
		abs.	*gain*	*abs.*	*gain*
deu.rst.pcc	95.58	96.28	-0.70	95.81	-0.23
eng.rst.gum	94.15	89.74	4.41	92.23	1.92
eng.rst.rstdt	96.64	91.41	5.23	94.59	2.05
eng.sdrt.stac	94.91	94.54	0.37	94.54	0.37
eus.rst.ert	90.46	91.01	-0.54	90.76	-0.30
fas.rst.prstc	92.94	92.99	-0.05	93.24	-0.30
fra.sdrt.annodis	90.02	88.80	1.22	88.48	1.54
nld.rst.nldt	95.97	95.48	0.50	95.11	0.86
por.rst.cstn	94.35	92.65	1.71	93.93	0.42
rus.rst.rrt	86.21	86.18	0.03	86.01	0.20
spa.rst.rststb	92.22	92.04	0.18	92.39	-0.17
spa.rst.sctb	82.48	84.21	-1.73	83.32	-0.84
zho.rst.sctb	83.34	84.87	-1.54	82.60	0.74
eng.pdtb.pdtb	92.02	87.72	4.30	82.42	9.60
tur.pdtb.tdb	94.11	94.02	0.10	93.54	0.57
zho.pdtb.cdtb	87.52	88.53	-1.01	88.14	-0.62
mean	91.43	90.65	0.78	90.45	0.99

Table 5: F_1 scores for ablations on gold treebanked data: next to normal scores from Table 4a, we report scores without handcrafted features, and without character embeddings and fastText static word embeddings, as well as the "gain" for each (non-ablated score – ablated score). Due to time constraints, ablations are based on *three* runs instead of the standard five.

Corpus	# Relations	Accuracy (w/ feats.)	Accuracy (w/o feats.)	Feature Gain
deu.rst.pcc	26	39.23	33.85	5.38
eng.pdtb.pdtb	23	74.44	75.63	-1.19
eng.rst.gum	23	66.76	62.65	5.55
eng.rst.rstdt	17	67.10	66.45	0.65
eng.sdrt.stac	16	65.03	59.67	5.36
eus.rst.ert	29	60.62	59.59	1.03
fra.sdrt.annodis	18	46.40	48.32	-1.92
nld.rst.nldt	32	55.21	52.15	3.06
por.rst.cstn	32	64.34	67.28	-2.94
rus.rst.rrt	22	66.44	65.46	0.98
spa.rst.rststb	29	54.23	54.23	0.00
spa.rst.sctb	25	66.04	61.01	5.03
tur.pdtb.tdb	23	60.09	57.58	2.51
zho.pdtb.cdtb	9	86.49	87.34	-0.85
zho.rst.sctb	26	64.15	64.15	0.00
fas.rst.prstc	17	52.53	51.18	1.35
mean		61.82	60.41	1.41

Table 6: Relation Classification Results. The score for each corpus is averaged over 5 runs. Also included is score *without* any hand-crafted features.

genre feature, but RST-DT and PDTB are homogeneous with respect to genre. We also note that GUM, RST-DT, and especially PDTB are large corpora, so perhaps the explanation lies in their size, but RRT is also very large and has multiple genres, yet handcrafted features led to nearly no gain on this dataset.

Turning now to the CWE-only ablation, we see a similar pattern: most corpora are only minorly affected by the inclusion of non-CWE embeddings, with a couple (GUM, RST-DT) showing a moderate gain of 2%, and one corpus (PDTB) showing an anomalous gain of 10%. Just as with the handcrafted feature ablation, it is difficult to know what could explain these corpora's divergent behavior. Ordinarily, static word embeddings might benefit small corpora with OOV items in the test set, since the embedding space will be stable in the unseen data – however PDTB is very large and homogeneous (newswire), making this explanation unlikely. Since no other corpus showed such a dramatic drop with non-CWE embeddings ablated, and since other CWE-based systems at DISRPT 2021 score around what our system would have scored if the drop had been more in line with what was observed for other corpora (2% drop, for a score in the low 90s, as was achieved by disCut and SegFormers), we speculate that the 10% drop observed here is due to some kind of implementation error or statistical fluke due to the nondeterminism of training models on GPUs, though the effect survives in the system reproduction on the Shared Task evaluators' machine.

In sum, our ablation study for segmentation and connective detection suggests that both handcrafted features and non-CWE embeddings are not silver bullets, though they are often helpful. Degradations were seen more often on smaller datasets, which perhaps indicates that in low-data situations these additional resources can serve more than anything as a source of overfitting. But both were on average responsible for a 1% gain,[d] which shows they are both useful, and invites the question of whether there might be even better handcrafted features, which could be tailored more accurately to properties of specific target languages and genres.

4.2 Relation Classification

Table 6 gives scores (averaged over 5 runs for each corpus) on relation classification on all 16 corpora. We include performance on all corpora without any hand-crafted features added in order to assess their utility, and we find that they appreciably boost performance, granting on average a 1.5% accuracy gain, with some of the biggest gains on small corpora with many labels like `deu.rst.pcc` (+5.38%) and `spa.rst.sctb` (+5.03%). Since difficulty of classification increases with number of labels, we also include the number of relation types for each

[d]Assuming that they can be treated independently, which is an idealization.

corpus in order to contextualize the scores. The `zho.pdtb.cdtb` corpus achieved the highest accuracy score, as there are only 9 relation types to classify,[e] and scores tend to be lower for corpora with many relations like `nld.rst.nldt`.

There is much variance in how much performance on each corpus was able to benefit from having additional features. Many of the corpora that had the largest gains are small, but this is not always the case: `tur.pdtb.tdb`, one of the larger corpora, has its score improved by 2.5%. On the other hand, while small corpora generally seem to benefit more from features, not all are able to: `fra.sdrt.annodis`, a small corpus, sees a degradation of 2% with features. We expect that much of the differential benefit of features is to be explained by the nature of the label-sets used in different corpora, and the available features. No two of these corpora use the exactly same label set, and label sets vary quite a bit in the linguistic phenomena that they encode and are sensitive to.

Additionally, different corpora have different features available, such as genre (GUM, RRT, RST-STB, PRSTC, SCTB – yes; PCC, PDTB, RST-DT, TDB – no), gold speaker information (STAC), discontinuity (Annodis, ERT, GUM, PDTB, RST-DT – yes; PCC, NLDT, STAC – no) etc., meaning that looking at gain across datasets is not comparing like with like. While some features are available for all corpora, such as distance, unit lengths, or position in document, others are restricted by framework, such as number of children, which is not relevant for PDTB-style data. A set of formalism-agnostic features (e.g. length_ratio, is_sentence, and the direction of the dependency head of the unit) were used for PDTB-style data across the board and were only effective for TDB: we hypothesized that the English PDTB dataset is so big that generic features do not add much value; for CDTB, as we found in our error analysis, the 9 relations sometimes are not very distinct from each other, and these generic features do not help with disambiguation in those cases.

Overall, a picture emerges with relations that is similar to the one that arose with segmentation and connective detection: features are helpful on the whole, slightly harmful in some cases, and especially helpful on some corpora. More work remains to be done in understanding the contribution of individual features and how these relate to the frameworks and data types available in each language.

5 Discussion

Figure 1 shows confusion matrices for common relations in the highest and lowest scoring EDU datasets, `eng.rst.gum` (GUM) and `eng.sdrt.stac` (STAC). Both panels reveal issues with over-prediction of the most common labels, which can be thought of as 'defaults': the most common ELABORATION in GUM and the second most common, COMMENT in STAC. The actual most common relation in STAC, QUESTION, does not suffer from false positives, likely due to a combination of the frequent and reliable question mark cue, *wh*-words or subject-verb inversion, combined with the availability of gold speaker and direction information (QUESTION only links units from different speakers, left to right). The same is true for QUESTION in GUM, which also obtained a comparatively high score. Conversely, rarer relations are hardly predicted, with ANTITHESIS in GUM being predicted for less than half of its true instances, and similarly for RESULT in STAC, suggesting a class imbalance problem, in particular given that both these relations are sometimes marked by overt discourse markers.

Although EDU datasets (RST/SDRT) do not distinguish explicit and implicit relations, analysis suggests that explicit signals are important. For GUM, the model scored high on medium-frequency relations with clear cues such as ATTRIBUTION, which are always signalled by attribution verbs such as *believe* and *say*. This also holds true for the `eng.rst.rstdt` corpus where ATTRIBUTION is the highest-scoring relation. GUM's ELABORATION and JOINT as well as SEQUENCE and JOINT are two pairs of relation labels that are most frequently confused with each other, as the former pair contains the two labels that are both overgeneralized and the latter contains the two labels that are both MULTINUCLEAR relation types that could be confusing when no explicit connective or lexical item indicating a sequential order of actions or events is present (Liu, 2019). Relations with relatively unambiguous markers, such as CONDITION, show good results in both GUM and STAC, indicating that even relatively rare relations can be identified

[e] Unlike the other two PDTB-style corpora (i.e. `eng.pdtb.pdtb` and `tur.pdtb.tdb`), where the predicted labels are truncated at Level-2 (e.g. TEMPORAL.ASYNCHRONOUS), the relation labels in `zho.pdtb.cdtb` only contain one level (e.g. TEMPORAL).

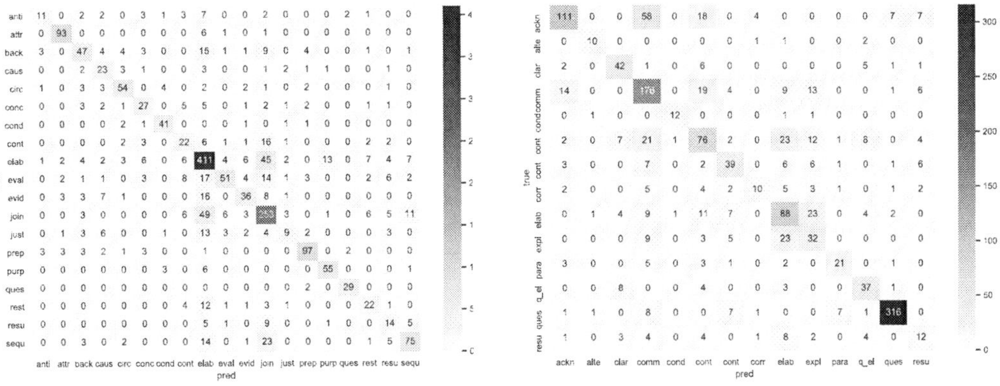

(a) eng.rst.gum (GUM)

(b) eng.sdrt.stac (STAC)

Figure 1: Confusion Matrices for Common Relations in the Highest and Lowest Scoring EDU Datasets.

if they are usually explicitly signalled.

Relations such as JUSTIFY, RESULT, and CAUSE scored low in both matrices as such instances in the test data often do not have explicit discourse markers to help understand the rhetorical relation between the units in context. In the presence of an ambiguous discourse marker, predictions prefer the relation that is more prototypically associated with that marker: for instance, the gold relation label for (1) is RESULT whereas the model classified it as SEQUENCE, likely due to the fact that the discourse marker *then* tends to be a strong signal for SEQUENCE indicating something sequential is involved.

(1) **Then** she lets go and falls . You scream . [GUM_fiction_falling]

In fact, if it were not the case that RST mandates a single outgoing relation per discourse unit, it would be possible to claim a concurrent sequential relation (likely to a previous unit) next to the annotated RESULT relation for the pair in the example (see Stede 2008 on concurrent relations in RST).

6 Conclusion

We have presented DisCoDisCo, a system for all tasks in the DISPRT 2021 Shared Task: EDU segmentation, connective detection, and relation classification. Our system relies on sequence tagging and sentence pair classification architectures powered by CWEs and supported by rich, handcrafted, instance-level features, such as position in the document, distance between units, gold speaker information, document metadata, and more.

Our results suggest that powerful pretrained language models are the main drivers of performance, with additional features providing small to medium improvements (with some exceptions, such as the high importance of speaker information for chat data as in STAC). For relation classification, CWEs pretrained using an NSP task proved to be superior.

Our error analysis suggests unsurprisingly that class imbalances, especially in the case of relations that tend to be implicit (i.e. lack overt lexical signals), lead to over-prediction of majority classes, suggesting a need for more training data for the minority ones. However, we are encouraged by improvements on datasets that were featured in the 2019 Shared Task (Zeldes et al., 2019), and the overall high scores obtained by the system across a range of datasets, all while including some correct predictions for relatively rare relations. We hope that the growing availability of annotated data, coupled with architectures that can harness pre-trained models, will lead to further improvements in the near future.

References

Nicholas Asher, Julie Hunter, Mathieu Morey, Benamara Farah, and Stergos Afantenos. 2016. Discourse structure and dialogue acts in multiparty dialogue: the STAC corpus. In *Proceedings of the Tenth International Conference on Language Resources and Evaluation (LREC'16)*, pages 2721–2727, Portorož, Slovenia. European Language Resources Association (ELRA).

Giuseppe Attardi, Daniele Sartiano, and Yu Zhang. 2021. DiaParser attentive dependency parser.

Piotr Bojanowski, Edouard Grave, Armand Joulin, and Tomas Mikolov. 2017. Enriching word vectors with subword information. *Transactions of the Association for Computational Linguistics*, 5:135–146.

Peter Bourgonje and Robin Schäfer. 2019. Multilingual and cross-genre discourse unit segmentation. In *Proceedings of the Workshop on Discourse Relation Parsing and Treebanking 2019*, pages 105–114, Minneapolis, MN. Association for Computational Linguistics.

Chloé Braud, Maximin Coavoux, and Anders Søgaard. 2017a. Cross-lingual RST discourse parsing. In *Proceedings of the 15th Conference of the European Chapter of the Association for Computational Linguistics: Volume 1, Long Papers*, pages 292–304, Valencia, Spain. Association for Computational Linguistics.

Chloé Braud, Ophélie Lacroix, and Anders Søgaard. 2017b. Does syntax help discourse segmentation? Not So Much. In *Proceedings of EMNLP 2017*, pages 2432–2442, Copenhagen.

Lynn Carlson, Daniel Marcu, and Mary Ellen Okurowski. 2003. Building a discourse-tagged corpus in the framework of Rhetorical Structure Theory. In *Current and New Directions in Discourse and Dialogue*, Text, Speech and Language Technology 22, pages 85–112. Kluwer, Dordrecht.

Jacob Devlin, Ming-Wei Chang, Kenton Lee, and Kristina Toutanova. 2019. BERT: Pre-training of deep bidirectional transformers for language understanding. In *Proceedings of the 2019 Conference of the North American Chapter of the Association for Computational Linguistics: Human Language Technologies, Volume 1 (Long and Short Papers)*, pages 4171–4186, Minneapolis, Minnesota. Association for Computational Linguistics.

Matt Gardner, Joel Grus, Mark Neumann, Oyvind Tafjord, Pradeep Dasigi, Nelson F. Liu, Matthew Peters, Michael Schmitz, and Luke S. Zettlemoyer. 2018. AllenNLP: A deep semantic natural language processing platform. In *Proceedings of ACL 2018*, pages 1–6, Melbourne, Australia.

Luke Gessler, Siyao Peng, Yang Liu, Yilun Zhu, Shabnam Behzad, and Amir Zeldes. 2020. AMALGUM - a free, balanced, multilayer English web corpus. In *Proceedings of LREC 2020*, pages 5267–5275, Marseille, France.

Grigorii Guz and Giuseppe Carenini. 2020. Coreference for discourse parsing: A neural approach. In *Proceedings of the First Workshop on Computational Approaches to Discourse*, pages 160–167, Online. Association for Computational Linguistics.

Hugo Hernault, Helmut Prendinger, David A. duVerle, and Mitsuru Ishizuka. 2010. HILDA: A discourse parser using support vector machine classification. *Dialogue and Discourse*, 1(3):1–33.

Matthew Honnibal, Ines Montani, Sofie Van Landeghem, and Adriane Boyd. 2020. spaCy: Industrial-strength Natural Language Processing in Python.

Dan Jurafsky and James H. Martin. 2020. *Speech and Language Processing*. https://web.stanford.edu/ jurafsky/slp3/.

Yusuke Kido and Akiko Aizawa. 2016. Discourse relation sense classification with two-step classifiers. In *Proceedings of the CoNLL-16 shared task*, pages 129–135, Berlin, Germany. Association for Computational Linguistics.

Najoung Kim, Song Feng, Chulaka Gunasekara, and Luis Lastras. 2020. Implicit discourse relation classification: We need to talk about evaluation. In *Proceedings of the 58th Annual Meeting of the Association for Computational Linguistics*, pages 5404–5414, Online. Association for Computational Linguistics.

Naoki Kobayashi, Tsutomu Hirao, Hidetaka Kamigaito, Manabu Okumura, and Masaaki Nagata. 2020. Top-down rst parsing utilizing granularity levels in documents. *Proceedings of the AAAI Conference on Artificial Intelligence*, 34(05):8099–8106.

Naoki Kobayashi, Tsutomu Hirao, Hidetaka Kamigaito, Manabu Okumura, and Masaaki Nagata. 2021. Improving neural RST parsing model with silver agreement subtrees. In *Proceedings of the 2021 Conference of the North American Chapter of the Association for Computational Linguistics: Human Language Technologies*, pages 1600–1612, Online. Association for Computational Linguistics.

Li Liang, Zheng Zhao, and Bonnie Webber. 2020. Extending implicit discourse relation recognition to the PDTB-3. In *Proceedings of the First Workshop on Computational Approaches to Discourse*, pages 135–147, Online. Association for Computational Linguistics.

Ziheng Lin, Hwee Tou Ng, and Min-Yen Kan. 2014. A pdtb-styled end-to-end discourse parser. *Natural Language Engineering*, 20(2):151–184.

Yang Liu. 2019. Beyond the Wall Street Journal: Anchoring and comparing discourse signals across genres. In *Proceedings of the Workshop on Discourse Relation Parsing and Treebanking 2019*, pages 72–81, Minneapolis, MN. Association for Computational Linguistics.

Yang Liu, Sujian Li, Xiaodong Zhang, and Zhifang Sui. 2016. Implicit discourse relation classification via multi-task neural networks. In *Proceedings of the Thirtieth AAAI Conference on Artificial Intelligence*, AAAI'16, page 2750–2756. AAAI Press.

Yinhan Liu, Myle Ott, Naman Goyal, Jingfei Du, Mandar Joshi, Danqi Chen, Omer Levy, Mike Lewis, Luke Zettlemoyer, and Veselin Stoyanov. 2019. RoBERTa: A robustly optimized BERT pretraining approach.

William C Mann and Sandra A Thompson. 1988. Rhetorical Structure Theory: Toward a Functional Theory of Text Organization. *Text-Interdisciplinary Journal for the Study of Discourse*, 8(3):243–281.

Daniel Marcu. 2000. *The Theory and Practice of Discourse Parsing and Summarization*. MIT Press, Cambridge, MA.

Mitchell P. Marcus, Beatrice Santorini, and Mary Ann Marcinkiewicz. 1993. Building a large annotated corpus of English: The Penn Treebank. *Special Issue on Using Large Corpora, Computational Linguistics*, 19(2):313–330.

Mathieu Morey, Philippe Muller, and Nicholas Asher. 2017. How much progress have we made on RST discourse parsing? a replication study of recent results on the RST-DT. In *Proceedings of the 2017 Conference on Empirical Methods in Natural Language Processing*, pages 1319–1324, Copenhagen, Denmark. Association for Computational Linguistics.

Philippe Muller, Chloé Braud, and Mathieu Morey. 2019. ToNy: Contextual embeddings for accurate multilingual discourse segmentation of full documents. In *Proceedings of Discourse Relation Treebanking and Parsing (DISRPT 2019)*, pages 115–124, Minneapolis, MN.

Thanh-Tung Nguyen, Xuan-Phi Nguyen, Shafiq Joty, and Xiaoli Li. 2021. RST parsing from scratch. In *Proceedings of the 2021 Conference of the North American Chapter of the Association for Computational Linguistics: Human Language Technologies*, pages 1613–1625, Online. Association for Computational Linguistics.

Adam Paszke, Sam Gross, Francisco Massa, Adam Lerer, James Bradbury, Gregory Chanan, Trevor Killeen, Zeming Lin, Natalia Gimelshein, Luca Antiga, Alban Desmaison, Andreas Kopf, Edward Yang, Zachary DeVito, Martin Raison, Alykhan Tejani, Sasank Chilamkurthy, Benoit Steiner, Lu Fang, Junjie Bai, and Soumith Chintala. 2019. Pytorch: An imperative style, high-performance deep learning library. In H. Wallach, H. Larochelle, A. Beygelzimer, F. d'Alché-Buc, E. Fox, and R. Garnett, editors, *Advances in Neural Information Processing Systems 32*, pages 8024–8035. Curran Associates, Inc.

Gary Patterson and Andrew Kehler. 2013. Predicting the presence of discourse connectives. In *Proceedings of EMNLP 2013*, pages 914–923.

Emily Pitler and Ani Nenkova. 2009. Using syntax to disambiguate explicit discourse connectives in text. In *Proceedings of the ACL-IJCNLP 2009 Conference Short Papers*, pages 13–16, Suntec, Singapore.

Balaji Polepalli Ramesh, Rashmi Prasad, Tim Miller, Brian Harrington, and Hong Yu. 2012. Automatic discourse connective detection in biomedical text. *Journal of the American Medical Informatics Association*, 19(5):800–808.

Rashmi Prasad, Nikhil Dinesh, Alan Lee, Eleni Miltsakaki, Livio Robaldo, Aravind Joshi, and Bonnie Webber. 2008. The Penn Discourse Treebank 2.0. In *Proceedings of the 6th International Conference on Language Resources and Evaluation (LREC 2008)*, pages 2961–2968, Marrakesh, Morocco.

Rashmi Prasad, Susan McRoy, Nadya Frid, Aravind Joshi, and Hong Yu. 2011. The Biomedical Discourse Relation Bank. *BMC bioinformatics*, 12(1):188.

Rashmi Prasad, Bonnie Webber, Alan Lee, and Aravind Joshi. 2019. Penn Discourse Treebank Version 3.0. LDC2019T05.

Peng Qi, Yuhao Zhang, Yuhui Zhang, Jason Bolton, and Christopher D. Manning. 2020. Stanza: A python natural language processing toolkit for many human languages. In *Proceedings of the 58th Annual Meeting of the Association for Computational Linguistics: System Demonstrations*, pages 101–108, Online. Association for Computational Linguistics.

Anna Rogers, Olga Kovaleva, and Anna Rumshisky. 2020. A primer in BERTology: What we know about how BERT works. *Transactions of the Association for Computational Linguistics*, 8:842–866.

Attapol Rutherford, Vera Demberg, and Nianwen Xue. 2017. A systematic study of neural discourse models for implicit discourse relation. In *Proceedings of the 15th Conference of the European Chapter of the Association for Computational Linguistics: Volume 1, Long Papers*, pages 281–291, Valencia, Spain. Association for Computational Linguistics.

Niko Schenk, Christian Chiarcos, Kathrin Donandt, Samuel Rönnqvist, Evgeny Stepanov, and Giuseppe Riccardi. 2016. Do we really need all those rich linguistic features? a neural network-based approach to implicit sense labeling. In *Proceedings of the CoNLL-16 shared task*, pages 41–49, Berlin, Germany. Association for Computational Linguistics.

Radu Soricut and Daniel Marcu. 2003. Sentence level discourse parsing using syntactic and lexical information. In *Proceedings of HLT-NAACL 2003*, pages 149–156, Edmonton.

Caroline Sporleder and Mirella Lapata. 2005. Discourse chunking and its application to sentence compression. In *Proceedings of EMNLP 2005*, pages 257-264, Vancouver.

Manfred Stede. 2008. Disambiguating rhetorical structure. *Research on Language and Computation*, 6(3):311–332.

Manfred Stede. 2011. Discourse Processing. *Synthesis Lectures on Human Language Technologies*, 4(3):1–165.

Huong Le Thanh, Geetha Abeysinghe, and Christian Huyck. 2004. Generating discourse structures for written text. In *Proceedings of COLING 2004*, pages 329–335, Geneva, Switzerland.

Jianxiang Wang and Man Lan. 2016. Two end-to-end shallow discourse parsers for English and Chinese in CoNLL-2016 shared task. In *Proceedings of the CoNLL-16 shared task*, pages 33–40, Berlin, Germany. Association for Computational Linguistics.

Yizhong Wang, Sujian Li, and Houfeng Wang. 2017. A two-stage parsing method for text-level discourse analysis. In *Proceedings of the 55th Annual Meeting of the Association for Computational Linguistics (Volume 2: Short Papers)*, pages 184–188, Vancouver, Canada. Association for Computational Linguistics.

Gregor Weiss and Marko Bajec. 2016. Discourse sense classification from scratch using focused RNNs. In *Proceedings of the CoNLL-16 shared task*, pages 50–54, Berlin, Germany. Association for Computational Linguistics.

Thomas Wolf, Lysandre Debut, Victor Sanh, Julien Chaumond, Clement Delangue, Anthony Moi, Pierric Cistac, Tim Rault, Remi Louf, Morgan Funtowicz, Joe Davison, Sam Shleifer, Patrick von Platen, Clara Ma, Yacine Jernite, Julien Plu, Canwen Xu, Teven Le Scao, Sylvain Gugger, Mariama Drame, Quentin Lhoest, and Alexander Rush. 2020. Transformers: State-of-the-art natural language processing. In *Proceedings of the 2020 Conference on Empirical Methods in Natural Language Processing: System Demonstrations*, pages 38–45, Online. Association for Computational Linguistics.

Nianwen Xue, Hwee Tou Ng, Sameer Pradhan, Rashmi Prasad, Christopher Bryant, and Attapol Rutherford. 2015. The CoNLL-2015 shared task on shallow discourse parsing. In *Proceedings of the Nineteenth Conference on Computational Natural Language Learning - Shared Task*, pages 1–16, Beijing, China. Association for Computational Linguistics.

Nianwen Xue, Hwee Tou Ng, Sameer Pradhan, Attapol Rutherford, Bonnie Webber, Chuan Wang, and Hongmin Wang. 2016. CoNLL 2016 shared task on multilingual shallow discourse parsing. In *Proceedings of the CoNLL-16 shared task*, pages 1–19, Berlin, Germany. Association for Computational Linguistics.

Zhilin Yang, Zihang Dai, Yiming Yang, Jaime Carbonell, Russ R Salakhutdinov, and Quoc V Le. 2019. Xlnet: Generalized autoregressive pretraining for language understanding. In *Advances in Neural Information Processing Systems*, volume 32. Curran Associates, Inc.

Yue Yu, Yilun Zhu, Yang Liu, Yan Liu, Siyao Peng, Mackenzie Gong, and Amir Zeldes. 2019. GumDrop at the DISRPT2019 shared task: A model stacking approach to discourse unit segmentation and connective detection. In *Proceedings of Discourse Relation Treebanking and Parsing (DISRPT 2019)*, pages 133–143, Minneapolis, MN.

Amir Zeldes. 2018. *Multilayer Corpus Studies*. Routledge Advances in Corpus Linguistics 22. Routledge, London.

Amir Zeldes, Debopam Das, Erick Galani Maziero, Juliano Antonio, and Mikel Iruskieta. 2019. The DISRPT 2019 shared task on elementary discourse unit segmentation and connective detection. In *Proceedings of the Workshop on Discourse Relation Parsing and Treebanking 2019*, pages 97–104, Minneapolis, MN. Association for Computational Linguistics.

Yingxue Zhang, Fandong Meng, Peng Li, Ping Jian, and Jie Zhou. 2021. Context tracking network: Graph-based context modeling for implicit discourse relation recognition. In *Proceedings of the 2021 Conference of the North American Chapter of the Association for Computational Linguistics: Human Language Technologies*, pages 1592–1599, Online. Association for Computational Linguistics.

Yuping Zhou, Jill Lu, Jennifer Zhang, and Nianwen Xue. 2014. Chinese Discourse Treebank 0.5. LDC2014T21.

Yuping Zhou and Nianwen Xue. 2012. PDTB-style discourse annotation of Chinese text. In *Proceedings of the 50th Annual Meeting of the Association for Computational Linguistics (Volume 1: Long Papers)*, pages 69–77, Jeju Island, Korea. Association for Computational Linguistics.